PRAISE FOR *My Wings at Sunset*

In *My Wings at Sunset*, Bob Lee has succeeded in weaving his recollections into a searching personal memoir. His ruminations modulate from jazz beat to Bach, from pilot to poet, and from family to future. His faith-based life has affected every aspect of his variegated roles: trumpet player, radio announcer, film producer, father, Navy pilot, husband, public relations liaison, and writer. All are self-examined by Lee and found to be the integral parts of a life fully lived.

Allie Clayton, film producer and artist

My Wings at Sunset is a moving story, filled with faith, with love and life, and with beauty and caring.

Mike Maus, former CBS radio reporter and PR executive

Bob Lee confesses that he loves to write—and he writes very well. We see the twentieth century through the eyes of this writer, film critic, movie producer, musician, and family man who carries with him a deep spiritual sensitivity. The result is both confession and proclamation—confession of the deepest foibles that humans encounter and proclamation of a faith that conquers all. Lee is still as creative and eager to encounter the world as he was when he flew in World War II or when he produced some of Protestantism's best films. *My Wings at Sunset* is a testament that will engage the mind and warm the heart.

William F. Fore, author and communication executive

Lee's memoir is like an old-time waltz. It is lyrical, sweet, and its rhythm continually moves the reader ahead. He was a mentor for my generation who showed us all how to use God's gift of creativity with conviction. With fascination, I followed him to war in the Pacific and a career of international scale.

Ann Hafften, religion journalist and author

My Wings at Sunset

Also by Robert E. A. Lee

Dear Elaine
Mathilda's Journey
The Joy of Bach
Popcorn and Parable (with Roger Kahle)
Martin Luther: The Reformation Years
Behind the Wall
Question 7

My Wings at Sunset

Living a Dream

A Communicator's Story

Robert E. A. Lee

iUniverse, Inc.
New York Lincoln Shanghai

My Wings at Sunset
Living a Dream

Copyright © 2007 by Robert E. A. Lee

All rights reserved. No part of this book may be used or reproduced by any means, graphic, electronic, or mechanical, including photocopying, recording, taping or by any information storage retrieval system without the written permission of the publisher except in the case of brief quotations embodied in critical articles and reviews.

iUniverse books may be ordered through booksellers or by contacting:

iUniverse
2021 Pine Lake Road, Suite 100
Lincoln, NE 68512
www.iuniverse.com
1-800-Authors (1-800-288-4677)

Because of the dynamic nature of the Internet, any Web addresses or links contained in this book may have changed since publication and may no longer be valid.

The views expressed in this work are solely those of the author and do not necessarily reflect the views of the publisher, and the publisher hereby disclaims any responsibility for them.

Front cover design by Sherwin Harris

ISBN: 978-0-595-44373-4 (pbk)
ISBN: 978-0-595-70391-3 (cloth)
ISBN: 978-0-595-88702-6 (ebk)

Printed in the United States of America

Dedicated to
Charles F. (Chuck) Nelson

Flying buddy and best friend
in the Pacific Theater
during World War II
all the way to today.

Keep your airspeed
Chuck, old boy!

Aging

Time is becoming more and more
Like sunrise and sunset
Less like the clock.

It is not the ding dong
Or the tick tock
That shapes my life

It is the flow of light
In the open air
That bids me rise
Or settle down to rest
Until light flows again.

Lois Langland

Contents

Introduction		1
1	Sunset	3
Poem	Who is He?	6
2	A Look in the Mirror	7
Poem	What's to Become of You?	11
3	A Child's Garden of Media	13
4	Follow the Leader	19
5	Pacific Odyssey	31
6	I Sang for My Father	43
7	Academic Discoveries	50
8	Snisket	60
9	Faith-based Life	74
10	Captured by Music	87
Poem	Musik's Mystery	94
11	On the Road with Martin Luther	95
12	Moviemaking Magic	105
13	Popcorn & Parable	117
14	Writing Therapy	124
Poem	Pear Tree Divided	126
Poem	Genetic Gratitude	128
Poem	Commuter's Sound Track	130
Poem	In the Tempo of Time	131
Poem	Sunset	132

15	God's Mysterious Gift	133
16	Celebration of Life	145
17	Sunset Reflections	154
Appendix	Bob's Gallery of Mentors	163
Song	My Wings at Sunset	173
Acknowledgments		175
About the Author		177

Introduction

Who wants to open himself honestly to public scrutiny? Yet what good is memoir sharing if it isn't candid and honest? It is the emotional, intellectual, and spiritual undressing that gives such storytelling both interest and integrity.

Perhaps the more fundamental question should be asked: Why? Who cares? I don't hear any calls for exposing the character who is I. Or is it *me*? "It's me, it's me, O Lord, standing in the need of prayer!"

A part of the answer is that *I* need to tell my story. I have lived and am still living a full and colorful life. I want the yarns I spin out here to connect somehow with you who are collecting (intentionally or not) your own treasury of experience. Maybe you will find stimulation in identifying with some of my memories. I hope you will laugh with me, perhaps cry with me, and even argue with or criticize me.

I look in the mirror. Even that takes some confidence for me these days. Who is the real person behind that image? Many are afraid to ask. But in telling my story in the following pages, I have discovered a lot about myself that I didn't know before. And maybe you will identify with some of it.

1 Sunset

I was lonesome for Elaine. She and I had been engaged a mere six months before, while I was in training as a cadet in Minneapolis. Now I was due to "engage the enemy" in a few weeks. Our squadron would move from California to active duty in the theater where our part of World War II was being fought—out over the Pacific and its islands, many of them still occupied by the enemy.

It was 1943 at Salton Sea, a salty, below-sea-level lake in the desert of California, across the mountains from San Diego and south of Palm Springs. The bleak site had been commandeered by the U.S. Navy as a flight training base for seaplanes. We had been reassigned there temporarily from the North Island Naval Air Station in San Diego Bay. Our main assignment was to practice take-offs and landings on this simulated ocean. Our large Catalina and Coronado flying boats were lumbering and vulnerable airborne instruments of what was then modern warfare.

The modest facilities included a room where I found a weather-beaten upright piano, almost in tune. I couldn't resist fiddling around with it. The lyrics and melody came straight from my heart. I couldn't easily sing my creation to Elaine, but I did write it out and mail it to her in Janesville, Wisconsin, where she was teaching music and English. And with the piano in her apartment she could make my meager scoring come alive. This typical 1940s pop-style song followed us through the years and became a standard in our private family repertoire.

> My wings at sunset
> are far from your view.
> My wings at sunset
> are flying for you.
>
> The clouds beyond me
> are part of my past.

> My wings at sunset
> come home now at last!
>
> I'm tired and weary
> from hours in the air.
> I'll sleep and dream, dear,
> of tomorrows we will share.
>
> My wings at sunset
> o'er foreign skies roam.
> My wings at sunset
> will carry me home!

The setting fed my loneliness. I had earned my "wings" just a few months before from the Navy's so-called "University of the Air" at Corpus Christi, Texas. There, from bays on the Gulf of Mexico, we had flown PBYs—two engine seaplanes, bulky boats that almost flew themselves. The Coronado, with its four engines, was larger and heavier—much more of a challenge to control, and this flyboy, a lowly Ensign, had much to learn.

While our squadron was mixing with the staff of the base, I hit it off with a lieutenant in operations. When I saw his name tag, Lt. Richard Haas, I thought he must be as Norwegian as I was, and probably from the Midwest. It turned out he was from Hollywood. He was a set designer for movies, and with my interest in film, I was curious about his work. He told me that our lake—Salton Sea—was the location for the popular wartime movie, *Wake Island*. He sketched out how Hollywood artists could transform this location into that Pacific isle, already the site of so much bloody action drama in the war. At the time, I couldn't have known that my own squadron would later participate in regaining U.S. control over Wake Island, a violent battle that would be costly for both sides. My war rehearsal at Salton Sea would be a preview of the real thing I would meet in the islands of the western Pacific.

I have often wondered if Haas survived the war and returned to filmmaking, but I never saw or heard about him again. And, of course, the war experience for many of us was that way. Which of our new friends would we ever meet again?

For me, World War II itself was also a kind of preview, a prototype for the modern life I was destined to live. Acceleration and change were dominant dynamics—seasoned with much hope for the future, tinged and shaded by a latent anxiety, and fueled by youthful vigor. There was a pervasive spirit of patriotism, naturally evoked without drum beating and flag waving—though such gestures were an inevitable part of the script. But like almost all my fellow sailors, soldiers, and marines (almost all men), I wore my uniform proudly. We pilots had gone through the formal ceremony on graduation to have wings pinned on our uniforms. For us, this was a proud emblem beyond the uniform itself. So the idea of wings in the song included both those I wore and those on the airplanes I flew.

My vision of the sunset was enhanced by the changing colors of the twilight fantasy that the Pacific horizon offered. When I saw the sunset over the ocean for the first time, I was awed by such extravagant and glorious brush strokes—a gift of God, the creative artist himself.

I thought ahead to what was in store for me toward the west.

> My wings at sunset
> o'er foreign skies roam.
> My wings at sunset
> will carry me home!

Navy Coronados in formation during World War II

Who is He?

Who is that old man who has come to live in my house?
Though he returned my stare this morning
as I stumbled from bed to bath
and beyond to dental brush,
I didn't know him.

Or did I?

Wizened, that weary face with wrinkled eyes,
not yet fully awakened, he studied me as much as I him.

I turned away, taking hairbrush to the tousled top of my head,
prompting me soon to seek the ministrations
of my Uzbek barber Boris (but not today, thanks),
and the stranger seemed to mock me by imitation.

Something about those gestures of his—
brushing teeth and hair, rinsing and squinting—
touched some memory cells as I peeked sideways
at the mirror image.

I didn't talk and he didn't say a word.
Finally I laughed.
He saw this and had to laugh, too.
We agreed: an absurd encounter!

Who is this presumptuous visitor,
this interloper who has come to share my digs,
this refugee from a gerontological documentary,
this uninvited senescent housemate?

Stop the clock! I declare a sick day.
I stumble back to my sack's security.

Who is he?

Lord, is it I?

2 A Look in the Mirror

Normally we don't see ourselves as others see us. The first cameras back in the early 1800s sparked a revolution. Before that time persons knew what they looked like only through a mirror image with its reversal of left and right. Suddenly it became possible to get an accurate self-image. Many may have been surprised, some pleased and proud, and others repelled.

When motion pictures came from Thomas Edison's laboratory at the end of the nineteenth century, the phenomenon of self-revelation was put in motion. Humans could finally sit back and watch themselves move—jerkily back then, but later more realistically. (It took a while to standardize the frames per second, and that's why we see agitated pedestrians speeding along in some archival footage.) Along came color, making moving film even more realistic. That was topped by sound, which was added and synchronized in the late 1920s.

I remember the first talkies. Even earlier, the phonograph had captured and recreated sound. A cousin of mine once demonstrated for me his cylinder music reproducing machine. I can still hear the song "Beautiful Ohio." I also remember early Bakelite recordings on platters (the logo "His Master's Voice" with the dog and the Victrola horn) with bouncing needles in scratchy grooves. And during World War II, I used audio tape recordings for the first time when we flyers practiced our radio lingo: "Roger … Wilco … Out!"

Television made its appearance before the war. I first saw it demonstrated in 1939 at the Minnesota State Fair, where KSTP from the Twin Cities had in its booth a live television camera. I stood in front of it and looked at my image on the small screen. TV began its fantastic growth after World War II, but only in black and white, with color sneaking into television broadcasting in the early 1950s. Video tape recording followed, first in black and white and then in color. As electronic miracles followed in bewildering succession, more and more we were permitted to see ourselves as others see us. Some of us shy away from these reflective inventions that reveal something of who we are. Not me. I am drawn to them because they stimulate my imagination.

So, who am I?

I am the surviving partner of a fifty-six year marriage with my loving and creative Elaine. I am the proud father of six splendid human beings: Peg, Barbara, Sigrid, Richard, Sylvia, and Paul. You will find them in supporting roles, woven into the warp and woof of this book's fabric, defining their father as well as themselves.

I confess: I like me! I am content. Not satisfied, to be sure. I struggle daily, as most of us do, with my own weaknesses. In college I was once slapped down with an accusation of being too cocky. I believe I learned from that good lesson, but I am happy with myself. Too many folks hate themselves or flail themselves with psychic penalties. At the other end of the spectrum, there also may be many folks who are too in love with themselves. I hope my place is safely in between. However, I do live with an attitude of gratitude. Each morning as I shake the sleep off and pause at the edge of my bed before starting my morning routine, I thank God for "life, health, and every good."

I am a Midwesterner from solid Norwegian-American immigrant stock. Most of my ancestors were agrarian pioneers who, half-way into the nineteenth century, dared to make the trans-Atlantic adventure. They were solid Lutherans, and this has been my own potent legacy since infant baptism. Our religion was considerably more conservative when I was growing up than it is now in my branch of that denomination. Today I find theological breathing room, and it wasn't always that way. But in matters of faith I still lean to the traditionalist foundations laid out by Herr Doktor Martinus Luther, the hero of the Reformation, who, as you will see, has managed to invade my life in curious ways.

I inherited a firm code of right and wrong. Familial love was there, but it was modestly implicit and hardly ever demonstrative. My father, Knute, was cozily warm and soft-spoken, with a prominent Scandinavian brogue and a love of singing, whereas my mother was an "in-charge" person. She had a good sense of humor that she kept well under control. We found her as family disciplinarian often brittle and abrasive. But, as her seven children testified by their words and their lives, she was a good mother. I loved writing my book about her: *Mathilda's Journey*—my way of honoring her remarkable life.

I was the youngest of the brood of five girls and two boys. How often I was identified as the "baby of the family"! I squirmed under that label, but in fact I was the luckiest of our tribe. I not only had my parents (very experienced in parenting, of course, by the time I arrived) as teachers, but my more senior siblings were even more effective mentors. I felt affirmed every day of my life in that family—and this affirmation has continued as a positive force throughout the balance of my life span.

The biblical injunction regarding a "good name" was inscribed in my memory. It came from a letter a fellow Navy pilot wrote to his parents from our Pacific island. My buddy Ensign Roland Johnson and I were together for hours at a time in the same patrol bomber. I was able to read his words because after he was killed in the war, his parents published a little booklet quoting from his letters. They sent a copy out to each of us in his squadron out there in the Pacific:

> I have been reading Proverbs 22. There is something in the opening lines that I have been thinking about today. *A good name is to be chosen rather than great riches, and favor is better than silver or gold.* This is to me both an inspiration and a reminder—I recall how many times I have met people and told them that I was your son and proudly observed their respect and approval of you.

I want to be known as one with a "good name." I don't just mean my surname, which derives from the Norwegian Li or Lie. My great grandfather's full name was Aad Ytrelie—reflecting the *outer lea* farm community near Aurland by the fjords in Norway. Nor by a "good name" do I merely mean my given names—all three of them: Robert Edward Alexander. Add Lee to that, and the initials spell REAL. (REALee?) But most of my friends and relatives call me Bob. I started using Bob when I was in college; I found that it gave me more immediate identification, particularly when I was on the air over KWLC, our Luther College radio station.

Johnny's proverbial "good name" suggests much more than a label. It is a profile, a portrait or a reputation—an appellation connoting respect.

Others, no doubt, could describe my personality more accurately than I. The only objective reflection of that came to me later in life when, like so many, I was subjected to the Myers-Briggs Profile, a psychic x-ray of emotions, perceptions, and judgments. Many career trainees will remember it. I found my test results fascinating and self-revealing. According to the resulting code ENFJ (Extrovert-Intuitive-Feeling-Judging, borrowed in great part from Jung's Typology Test), persons like me are likely to have their personality described this way:

> They look at things with their intuition rather than their senses, hence are mainly interested in seeing the possibilities beyond what is present or obvious or known. Intuition heightens their

understanding, long-range vision, insight, curiosity about new ideas, love of books, and tolerance for theory.

They are likely to have a gift of expression, but may use it in speaking to audiences rather than in writing. Interest in possibilities for people attracts them often to counseling in the fields of career choice or personal development.

Now, later in life, writing as gift and penchant has a greater priority than does speaking. Yet there was a time when I was a broadcaster that "speaking to audiences" fit perfectly. Overall, I now see the ENFJ description is pretty much on target.

I would argue that anyone who chooses a career as a professional communicator has an extrovertial compulsion similar to mine to share information, ideas, stories, or artistic creations and will work hard at the process. Communication efforts are often painfully complicated, but satisfaction comes in and with the frustration and struggle. And the rewards are largely the joy of connecting successfully with the recipients—the readers and listeners "out there"—as well as the nourishing of one's ego by some credit lines. What pleasure to hear "I read your piece" or "I heard you on the air!"

So who is the real person behind the image in my mirror? I see someone who enjoys introspection, who likes a certain amount of recognition, who loves the craft of communication, who treasures a rich family life, to whom a good name is important, and whose vision is full of hope and expectation. Now that I look back on the life I have lived—and I look back a lot these days—I realize I survived many unmet goals, dreams that proved to be "pie in the sky." But I weep not at such ephemeral disappointments. Instead, I focus on the richness, the stimulation, the learning, the gifts of grace and talent, and the love that has surrounded me through decades. For all these, and for life itself, I give thanks.

What's to Become of You?

What's to become of you,
little boy, standing there
looking dourly enigmatic,
unintentionally dramatic?
Your years are few,
more than one, but less than two.
I see you stand there so erect:
"Good boy!"—yes, so correct.
Do you also walk, begin to talk?

Your outlook's straight,
your vision's long,
serious, somber—rather strong,
yet something seems a wee bit wrong.

Worried perhaps of what's ahead:
school, college, work and war,
marriage, family, earning bread?

You'll hear sisters, mothers, others say
as you talk and sing and write and play,
"Little guy, what's to become of you?"
thinking ahead to a future day.

Don't worry, kid,
I know the answer, see—
strange as it has come to be:
your "you" is now my "me."

Robert Edward Alexander Lee—
you've grown from two to eighty-three!

3 A Child's Garden of Media

Radio and I grew up together in the 1920s. In our Spring Grove home, our first Atwater-Kent receiver had three dials, each having to be fine-tuned to the same frequency. It was powered by an automobile battery, which my father placed under the receiver. We would gather in the living room to be enthralled with music from Chicago and voices from New York. In the bedroom I shared with my older brother, I would drop an aerial wire out the window so that, by fidgeting with my own mail-order crystal set, I could hear faint music through a headset.

Author in early 1930s dreaming of a media career

It was a wonderful era. In the midst of the Depression of the 1930s we were unabashedly awe-struck by this magic device that translated invisible ether waves into sound. We regularly picked up WLW in Cincinnati, a so-called clear channel; we found it difficult to avoid Dr. John Brinkley's powerful transmitter XEL down on the Mexican border at Del Rio, Texas, touting dubious cancer cures and goat-gland sex therapy.

My dream of becoming a radio announcer began, I think, from hearing the velvet baritone of Andre Baruch enter our home from WGN in Chicago. I also loved tuning in Boake Carter each evening with news from New York by way of LaCrosse, Wisconsin, or Cedar Rapids, Iowa. My father had built a little shelf by the kitchen door for the arch-shaped Philco. It was placed high enough so that, as a child, I had to stand on a stool to see the dial.

The daily Boake Carter newscast was introduced by a golden-toned announcer who identified himself by saying, "This is Eric Rolfe." But I knew his real name was Rolf Ylvisaker, the son of a well-known preacher who had visited our town. If Rolfe (or even Rolf) could make it to the top in radio, coming as he did from the same Norwegian-American Lutheran enclave in the Midwest that had bred me, maybe I could make it too.

We had no radio station in Spring Grove. LaCrosse, the Mississippi River city thirty miles east of us, sent us its strong AM signal from WKBH (FM had not yet been introduced). I'll always remember the day my mother's voice came to us from that station. My own mother! My sisters ushered us all into the kitchen so that we could hear every word of her talk for the American Red Cross. During the Great Depression, when many people had no money for basic necessities, she was in charge of food and clothing distribution in our community. I now believe she may have read from a canned script furnished by the Red Cross. No matter. Mom made it hers. After all, as the one doling out the supplies from our home, she *was* the Red Cross in our town.

I would not stand in front of a live microphone until high school, when our male quartet finally got its chance to sing over the air. I was sure everyone in the world—my world at least—was listening. Yet few folks commented on our broadcast.

Film also got into my blood early. For my sixth birthday my father bought me a mail-order movie projector. My brother Bill, five years my senior, arranged this, perhaps as much for his own pleasure as mine. The magic device came with a short film loop of Charlie Chaplin and his reluctant donkey. We showed it over and over again in the darkness of our basement against a white bed sheet hung over a clothesline. I wore a button that said I was the

"Operator" (I turned the crank—it wasn't an electric model), and Bill's button claimed for him the title, "Manager." This was the Lee theater, Phase I.

My romance with cinema was clinched when I was given the job of pulling my little red wagon up to the train depot to pick up the cans of film (35 mm silent reels) and deliver them to the projection booth at the high school auditorium across the street from our house. My payment was a free pass to the movie of the week. I remember Rin Tin Tin and Tom Mix and Clara Bow. These great silent films, enhanced by a piano score sometimes performed by my sister Juliet, told me of a world far from Spring Grove.

That's when I decided I wanted to be a performer. All my siblings had outgrown their interest in what we always called the "playhouse." It was attached to a woodshed and a garage. In the earlier days when our family had chickens, the playhouse was the chicken coop. There was a still a tiny trap-door exit for the fowl at the rear of the narrow room. But it was ideal for a small theater. So some neighbor kids and I built a stage across the far end, put up a curtain, and put on our own shows for whatever audience we could cajole into coming. This was the Lee theater, Phase II.

I had no trouble gaining a captive audience for my make-believe radio broadcasts. We had a hot air furnace with a single register on the floor of our living room (sometimes called the parlor or front room). I would set up my studio in the cellar next to the furnace. We had an old crank-up phonograph, and my sisters had some 78 rpm records of popular songs.

To spin records and ad-lib my way through my own home-style pretend radio show, I would open the little furnace door that gave air flow access to the floor above. When I was tired of giving announcer-like spiels of news, weather, gossip, and general chit-chat (after all, it was a *hot air* furnace), I would sing. I loved to sing and was pretty good at it. My family would show me off when guests were present. They would prompt me to do my routine in the cellar and would laugh and applaud upstairs. It never occurred to me then that maybe they were laughing at me rather than affirming me.

I had begun performing before a larger public at an early age. As the baby in the family, I was frequently manipulated by the others to entertain. First it was in a kindergarten toy symphony performing between acts of the senior class play at our high school. Then, with Juliet providing piano accompaniment to any song I chose, I offered solos on my first musical instrument—the comb! Humming through vibrating paper against the tines of a comb gave me a talent without having to practice scales, learn fingering or read music.

My mother, however, did teach me early on how to read notes and pick out melodies and chords on the piano. When Bill began playing cornet, he taught me the basics. He decided we should play trumpet duets, with Juliet at the piano. We played at church programs and at ice cream socials. Later I took some piano lessons and trumpet lessons. Much of this was wasted because I got by without having to practice.

Even the telegraph was part of my linkage to the outside world. My father hauled freight from the train station to the merchants, and I would often go with him to the depot to help load boxes and, later, to get the freight bills which Dad would have to collect. The depot agent became a friend of mine. I loved to watch him beat out messages in code with his hand on the click-clacker. And when the wires came in, I watched in awe as he typed out the words as fast as they clicked through. In World War II as a part of ground-school training I, too, had to learn to send messages in Morse code (dah dit dit dah and all that), and my thoughts went back to those childhood moments with Mr. Sturm at the Milwaukee Railroad depot in my hometown.

We had a small portable Corona typewriter at our house. I am sure my father got it second-hand in a trade of some kind. I used it constantly and taught myself to type—only it wasn't quite a standard keyboard, so later in high school I had to learn all over again the right way—touch typing. Today I think through my fingers and can barely recall that early initiation into typing.

I started my journalism career by publishing The Lee Journal. Essentially it was my own re-write of the news in the newspapers and magazines and what I had heard on the radio. And I would include reporting of local news as it happened. No one outside our family subscribed.

This led to my first paying job writing for publication. Perk Steffan, the editor of the weekly paper in the neighboring town, offered me the chance to submit Spring Grove news items to his paper, the *Caledonia Journal*. I had no idea why he selected me. Later I figured out that, because my oldest sister Sylvia was a friend of his, she must have told him about me. He was a "perky" kind of guy with that keen sense of integrity so many small town editors have. He was actually willing to pay me five cents a word—or was it five cents a line? Or a column inch? For a kid during the Depression, those several dollars a month were important. It was the first time I got paid for something.

Was I in junior high school or in senior high at the time? I was just a kid, anyway. My beat included going to our town's telephone operator; Genora was her wonderful name, and she *was* wonderful. She took a personal interest in me. She wrote for the *Winona Republican Herald*, a daily paper with many subscribers in our town. She seemed to respect me as a colleague and willingly shared her collection of items as I stood by her switchboard. Our conversation was constantly interrupted by her answering calls and chatting with people who had to go through her "central" to get connected with their neighbors or with Long Distance. I knew very well how she knew so much local gossip. She sat at the communication hub of our town.

My second local source, Anna Gilbertson, wrote Spring Grove news for another daily, the *LaCrosse Tribune*. She worked at a portrait studio and never seemed too busy to help me. Sometimes I would wait and watch her pose a bride and groom or a family against the painted Italian backdrop.

My mother could write but she couldn't type. So she had me type her manuscript for a history she wrote. She told the story of the various auxiliary organizations that were spawned by our local Lutheran parish. I also typed material she prepared for the history of Houston County. It was good practice. I shared the excitement of seeing the galleys come back from the printer with the sweet smell of ink still flavoring the enamel-stock pages.

Recording was an exotic art for us in those pre-World War II days. The first time I was in on a recording was as a member of our high school chorus as we performed at a state music festival. I had never heard my own voice. I didn't recognize my tenor contribution, but it was nevertheless stimulating to know I was in there somewhere.

Once I got to college I headed for the radio station as if I always knew that was where I belonged. It was a primitive place: no recording equipment during that first year. But even before I learned how I sounded on the air, I had some feedback from the professor (a biologist) who was in charge of the campus station. He stopped his car one day as he saw me walking along the campus, rolled down his window and called me over.

"I heard you on the air this morning," he said, smiling. "You should know you have a very good radio voice. Make the most of it!"

With the benefit of hindsight I see my childhood as a laboratory of motivating experience in media. For me it had a magic that became part of my dream for the future.

I predicted this in high school. A favorite teacher, Georgia Garlid, gave us an English assignment. She told us to write our biography in advance of our living it: tell about what you think your career will be.

Often I recall that assignment. I wrote that I would be heard on radio as an announcer (I was) and a singer (I was), that I would produce movies (I did) and maybe act in them (I didn't), and that I would write books (I did and am). I knew nothing then of television or video (this was 1938), but my vision expanded to include them when they came along.

In first grade I fell in love with my religion teacher, Gladys Hanson. Many years later she wrote to me from Madagascar where she had gone to be a missionary. Her letter told me that she and her husband were listening one day to shortwave, and on the program coming from HCJB, "The Voice of the Andes" in Quito, Ecuador, she heard a name she knew. My name. She was hearing the radio program I had created, called "Children's Chapel."

What great feedback for her—to know that the little boy in her first grade class was now sending back to her the same Bible stories over radio that she had taught him.

And what great feedback for me—to know that my childhood dream was truly being lifted up and out across mountains, oceans, and continents to a far-off listener who remembered my name!

4 Follow the Leader

It was a Wednesday and Saturday night ritual in our little Minnesota town: people were shopping and gathering in clusters to visit on Main Street. Farmers and their families who had come to town to "trade," as they called it, had doubled the village population. I was hanging out (we didn't call it that then but that's just what it was) downtown or uptown, depending on how you looked at the one street of stores along Route 44 that bisected the town east to west.

I was sitting on the bronze lion in front of Fladager's Clothing Store. My brother suddenly appeared. "You gotta come home, Robin," he announced. "You're going to Decorah tomorrow morning. I've got you a job at Luther!"

He didn't ask me. He told me. The biggest decision of my life, as it turned out, wasn't something I decided. My brother decided.

The lion that launched a college education—now moved to City Park in Spring Grove

Bill decided I should enroll at Luther College, the same nearby Iowa institution from which he had recently graduated. It was 1938, and the Depression had all but drained me of hope that there might be a college education in my future. The Lee family had no money. How could I afford college? I had finished high school a few weeks before. I had no idea what I would do next.

Luther College changed my life. It meant that I could pursue my music, play in the band, sing in the choir, and also realize my childhood dream of becoming a radio announcer, program host, and singer. But most of all it was the place where I met my wife, Elaine.

But brother Bill had begun changing my life much earlier.

I grew up in his shadow. He was six years older and could dominate me most of the time—and did. It wasn't until much later that we became friends on the same level of young-adult maturity.

He seemed to sense that he was responsible for me. Our five sisters were, of course, part of the family equation. My sister Julie was a kind of deputy mother or designated nanny for me. But Bill assumed the role of his brother's keeper. Oh, we fought, and I resisted his manipulations as far as I could. But he would somehow get me to do his will. When he advertised his services washing and waxing cars I was commandeered as his assistant, and I hated every minute of it. He led the way with hoe and spade to the huge garden our mother had arranged as the source of much food for our huge family. He was the master, and I was the slave—or so it seemed to me.

My brother insisted I learn to milk a cow; soon I graduated from tag-along companion to bovine finder and fetcher; it wasn't long before it was I who was squirting warm milk into the pail.

He taught me to fly a kite, split wood, drive a car, and play the trumpet. It was the start of a continuing game of follow the leader.

He forced me to drive a car when I was eight years old. I had never driven before and could hardly see over the steering wheel of his topless Model T Ford—it was probably one of the fruits of a trade my bartering father had made. Bill's car had stalled that day on his way home from nearby Blackhammer. No doubt he ran out of gas. He almost made it home; the breakdown was only three-quarters of a mile away, just beyond the cemetery. He walked (and, very possibly, ran) back home. He got a can of gas and fetched me to accompany him back in another of our several very-used cars, probably the heavy old Graham Paige.

It didn't take him long to refuel and get his rickety Ford started. He had me sit and operate the gas and choke levers while he cranked the engine so it sputtered and came alive. Then he told me I would drive it home. He would drive the Paige home at the same time—well, more or less at the same time. His plan was to get me started on the way, then he would race to the other vehicle and park down the road a ways. He knew the intersection from the country road to the main highway would be tricky, so he parked up ahead and then raced back to make sure I didn't turn into any traffic. He did this four or five times before we got home. The next precarious maneuver was soon after entering our village: the left turn against traffic onto the street that led to our house. But we made it okay and were soon in sight of the Lee house. The folks at home came out on the porch because someone called out that Bill's car was coming up the street with no driver, and Bill himself was running after it! I was so short they couldn't see me driving—and if they had, they would have been even more shocked.

Well, it made a good family story that has been repeated often and improved upon for dramatic effect. The kid brother was hugged and praised and congratulated. The older brother was chastised by his scolding mother and sisters. Our dad wasn't there to see it. He would have laughed loudest, I am sure.

Bill decided that I should be a Boy Scout and ushered me into his league as a Tenderfoot. And, as a perk from his and my trumpet playing, he got me a job one summer at Scout Camp as bugler. That meant I could work for my board and room and still enjoy the same privileges that paying campers had, while my brother pursued—and succeeded in earning—his prized Eagle Scout honor.

At home we slept in the same bed also, as many siblings did then. Our small single bed had springs that had long since lost their firmness and tension. So we sank together into the middle trough. Somehow we managed this awkward sleeping arrangement until he left for college.

Bill might have taught me about sex also, but in our conservatively religious family that was almost out of bounds to think about, to say nothing of talking about. One time he took me aside in our bedroom and, in all seriousness, he made me pull down my pants and underwear for what the Navy later would later tell me was a "short-arm inspection." He gave me the briefest of lectures on keeping clean because, while he had been circumcised, he discovered I had not been. No one else would have told me that, I'm sure. Certainly not my father or, heaven forbid, my mother.

Between my junior and senior years at Luther College, Bill was teaching music and directing high school band in Glasgow, Montana. He invited me to come out to spend a few days with him. He had a car. I did not. So I hitchhiked out from Decorah, Iowa, to Montana.

It was in Montana that I discovered that he smoked. And he discovered that I did. Wow! This was a new experience: our lying together on his bed talking about life and smoking one cigarette after the other. But no beer or wine or anything like that. And smoking? We both gave it up decades ago.

He arranged for me to have my first airplane ride. He was already taking a few private and unofficial flying lessons from a friend. He had his friend give me an aerial tour. I felt we were not moving, but simply floating. Even though we had the purring of the engine and propeller, I liked the sensation of being free of the usual earthly impediments like the sound of tires, the honking of horns, and the zooming of passing cars. I didn't admit to him that I wasn't exactly ecstatic about this adventure, as I'm sure he was more excited than I.

We traveled one summer weekend in 1941 in his car to a large Lutheran youth convention in Billings, Montana. He couldn't leave Glasgow until midnight because he had to play at a dance. He played trumpet and clarinet and maybe even trombone. He enjoyed every minute. And so did I, listening to my brother, the jazz musician. After the dance, we drove all the night through and came into Billings at dawn to join the thousands of young people at the convention.

Later that year of 1941, he left to join the Navy. I was against it. My letters to him are almost embarrassing to me now, as I argued from a pacifist position. He was a patriot, and the United States was headed into war, and he knew it and wanted to be a part of it. He wanted badly to fly an airplane for his country. It fit his macho personality. After all, he was the teenager in our hometown who would ride his motorcycle down Main Street and, while doing it, stand up on the seat. Bill got into a lot of trouble doing stunts like that. His kid brother the pacifist never did.

When our country finally was plunged into World War II at Pearl Harbor on the famed "Day of Infamy" that year, Bill was in Navy flight school in Corpus Christi, Texas. And Bob had only six months left of college before his graduation with a B.A. degree.

The old follow-the-leader pattern was still operative in those early days of the war. December 7, 1941, was conversion day for Bob, who suddenly found pacifism untenable. So, with the magnetic model of older brother pulling me along, I, too, became a naval aviator.

We didn't see much of each other while in uniform. We did manage in the summer of 1944 to connect on a date for my wedding so he could be my best man. (Elaine always felt I was more concerned about his being there than about her family's finding that date convenient.)

He flew for the Navy in the Pacific. I followed and flew in the Pacific also. Different types of planes. Different duty. Same war. One time he hitch-hiked two thousand miles (without authorization) to visit me aboard our seaplane tender in a lagoon at Okinawa. How could he even find me with all the secrecy that the Navy tried to maintain? But he came, and we had a terrific time as two young Navy pilots who happened to be brothers. It wasn't difficult to arrange a couple of enemy air raids for him. The Kamikaze planes (suicide bombers) came almost daily. And on his way back to Saipan he had another adventure that demonstrated his living on the edge: the PBM seaplane in which he was a passenger lost an engine but was able to limp back home.

We tried hard to keep in touch with one another. We had a flurry of letters back and forth, many having to be forwarded because the FPO (Fleet Post Office) had a mammoth job of keeping track of a constantly shuffling deployment of units. The first paragraphs of most letters, once they caught up with us, were devoted to apologies for not writing sooner. As it was, the actual correspondence under wartime circumstances was almost miraculous. What a difference e-mail would have made in those early 1940s.

He wrote me from Pearl Harbor that since first receiving his wings nine months earlier, he had recorded in his log book only about 730 hours of flying, but "it was enough to kick an OS [his observation seaplane] around!" He wrote that he and his buddy Jim Nifong volunteered for an assignment that took them to New Caledonia, near Australia, where the Navy had established a big fleet center. They volunteered for this in spite of what he described as "a standing rule" in the Navy: "Keep your eyes, ears, and bowels open and your mouth shut, and don't volunteer for a thing!"

As it turned out, that volunteer gesture led to his getting the coveted Navy Cross medal, one of the most prestigious our government could bestow. The Navy publicized his medal in his hometown area, naturally, and his photo and a story about it flooded the Upper Midwest newspapers. It was all due to his being the key flyer to sink a Japanese submarine. A year later, when I was out in the Pacific as well, I happened to spot a story in the bulletin sent throughout the system by COM AIR CENPAC (Central Pacific Air Command) about characteristics of Japanese submarines. I wrote him immediately:

> If you can get ahold of a copy (#A8/FF12/25-dch) by all means do. Here's why: on page 3 there is a caption "Here's How They Got a Big One" and what follows is the account of the action that merited you the Navy Cross. I learned that it was "More than a usual prize, since survivors taken after the sinking identified the I-17 as the sub which shelled the oil refinery at Galeta, California in February 1942 …" Also that from these survivors was obtained important information on the I-17 previously not known. You can imagine how good it

makes me feel to read something like this that has been distributed throughout the Pacific fleet. What a coincidence to find it!

As I look back on those days when we were both in the Pacific and flying for the Navy, the odds of our connecting at all seem kind of spooky. It's like the time years later when I was living and working in New York, and he was living in Brooklyn and studying at Columbia for his doctorate. One day at the subway station at Times Square, I was coming from Penn Station, where my Long Island train terminates. As our subway car pulled into the station, I stood at the door to exit; there was a group waiting to enter. When the door opened, the first person I saw waiting was Bill. He had come on the subway from Brooklyn and was changing trains. Of all the tens of thousands of subway passengers at that morning rush hour, here was my brother!

During the war I sometimes felt he was known all over the Pacific. At least three times I ran into friends of his I had never seen before. Once in San Diego's Naval Air Station in the B.O.Q. (bachelor officers' quarters) hallway, a Lt. Hensley across the hall came out of his room as I came out of mine. He looked at my name on my jacket and asked, "Do you know Bill Lee?" They had flown together in New Caledonia, and Bill had told him about me.

Lee brothers commissioned as Navy flyers

Another time at the officer's club bar at Johnston Island the fellow next to me turned out to be a friend of my brother's with whom Bill flew patrols over the ocean from Coos Bay, Oregon. His question was essentially the same: "Do you know a flyer we call Ace Lee?" He was the same Tom Moore who became a programming executive at both CBS and ABC. He was the one who suggested to my writer friend Allan Sloane that he check on the story of "Buzz Boy" for one of his *Navy Log* scripts. It was Bill's story. In the 1950s our family watched on television the saga of a brash young flyer who buzzed the football stadium and flew under a bridge, bringing him a strong reprimand from the admiral. I thought the script was good but the production lousy, so I was both proud and disappointed at the same time.

And one time at Saipan I was chatting with the executive officer of a small ship in the harbor. When he heard my name was Lee, he said, "You must be Newt Lee's brother!" Did we look alike or sound alike? I had never thought so.

I was also surprised to discover we were both in Hawaii at the same time. It was immediately after VJ Day. Not having heard from him for months, I didn't even know whether or not he was still alive. On arrival I phoned some Honolulu friends of his and discovered that he had phoned them also. I located him by phone aboard a carrier at Pearl Harbor, and he commandeered transportation and came to me at Kaneohe Naval Air Station, across the island of Oahu. We had several more precious days together.

Only then did I learn that he had had to ditch his own fighter plane off the coast of Japan following a raid by the group he was leading. He had used almost all his fuel circling his wingman, who was bobbing in the Inland Sea after being shot down. Finally he had to abandon the vigil and head for a so-called "Dumbo" U.S. submarine on rescue duty off shore. As we compared notes, I realized that while flying patrol over that same territory I had made radio contact with that very same sub without knowing that he was aboard.

Looking back, I feel grateful that I was able to tell him directly during the war how indebted I was to him for being my mentor since childhood. I recently came across the following letter penned by me in 1943:

> Mother was so thrilled to receive your letter—so beautifully and appropriately timed—on Christmas Eve.
>
> I guess you know I think you are well nigh perfect as a brother and as a man. I can thank you for a host of things—your early efforts in giving me a training in many things, your interest and support in seeing me through college, your inspiration and example so necessary for me to make the grade as a naval aviator—yes, for all

these I shall be eternally grateful. <u>But</u>, what I thank you most for is your being such a wonderful man—so staunch a Christian character and personality. I pray that I may have the strength to live up to the example you have given me.

It may sound as if I completely idolized my brother. Without detracting from his amazing strengths and his reputation for outrageous generosity, my appraisal would not be balanced if his rough edges and his sometimes stubborn impetuosity were not a part of the mysterious equation that explains Bill's life. In the last decades of his journey, he appeared to us to have lost some of his joy of life. When we called from the East Coast, we heard his famous (or infamous) laugh exploding less and less frequently. He seemed to have soured on society. I sensed he was unhappy. His tone and comments often seemed judgmental. We argued religion and politics. Over the years he had become more conservative while I became more liberal. As an ordained pastor and religion teacher with an earned doctor's degree, he had strong opinions on religious issues. One of the major theological movements in the last half of the twentieth century was called biblical criticism. His outspoken views against that made him controversial at Luther College and at Pacific Lutheran, both schools where he taught. He found his tenure at the Lutheran Bible Institute more compatible with his positions. I finally had to avoid controversial topics in our dialogues, whether by letter, phone, or in person. In retrospect I now recognize that his developing Alzheimer's ate away at his spirit's buoyancy for almost ten years before the end.

As he struggled with memory and reality in those last years, he may not have remembered my life-long deep love for him. He also may have forgotten his wartime hopes and dreams regarding his and my careers. I remember his writing to me as early as 1943:

> Do you still ever think that maybe you and I might go to the sem some day? Maybe a pipe dream but sometimes dreams come true. I think a lot about it, although time alone will tell.

Again, I dip into our war-time correspondence for my words of appreciation so sincerely meant:

> Whenever I get a letter from you I read it with intense, child-like eagerness and then re-read it betimes.

> I know that it's inescapably apparent, but I wonder if you realize fully just how much you have influenced my life and, for that matter, still do. I realize that I have followed a path that you have blazed—tracking, as it were, a course that you have charted and flown. Now you have done some long-range planning and have charted a definite course toward becoming a Lutheran minister after the war. You are wondering if I, again, will follow suit …
>
> Frankly, I am wondering too. Ever since the day that I, as a candidate for confirmation, went into the sacristy of our home church, as it was my turn for a routine conference with Pastor Mick, and after wishing me God's blessing in life et al., he said as he clasped my hand, "I hope sometime you will consider the ministry." Ever since then, through college where more avid influences and inspirations were my lot, through the gamut of ups and downs in the Navy, and up to the present, I have pondered that very thought.

One time later, after the war, we were on a bus together at night returning from our hometown to the Twin Cities of Minnesota, where Bill was a Lutheran seminary student and I was a radio announcer. He didn't pressure me at all but it was clear that he wanted me to consider following him into the ministry as an ordained clergyman.

He went on to a colorful and distinguished career as a Lutheran pastor, chaplain to construction crews in the Arctic, college religion teacher, and author. Those who heard his sermons, attended his lectures, and read his books did not know him as Bill, as he was always known within our family. His public moniker was Knute W. D. Lee.

I had followed him through boyhood, college, and halfway around the world as a Navy flyer, but now my answer had to be no. My vision was different. I explained to Bill that I would have a "ministry" also, but as a Christian layman, not as a pastor. I saw myself as a communicator. As it turned out, most of my career was as a broadcaster and film producer for the same national church body in which brother Bill himself served as pastor and professor.

One October weekend in the 1970s, we arranged to meet back in our hometown. My brother had a strong emotional need to be there and wanted me to share it. He flew in from the West Coast and I from the East Coast. He had convinced me that we could combine a joint visit to our aging mother, then in her nineties, with a walking tour around the edge of the small village where we grew up, down in the southeastern corner of the state. He wanted badly to rediscover the ridges, valleys, woods, creeks, meadows, and corn fields where he—and, to a lesser extent, I—had hiked and played, tried building dams along the springs and groves, and camped out with fellow Cubs and Boy Scouts. These places had haunted his dreams. It sounded okay—interesting but for me not compelling. I agreed mostly because he asked me to meet him there and it would be like "following the leader," wouldn't it?

After a big (too big) breakfast at our mother's table, we started out to find some trails south of town. When I heard him tick off the names of nearby houses and farms and noticed his recognizing this or that stand of trees, this little roadway, that winding stream, I came to realize how deeply our hometown had been imprinted on his boyhood experience. I envied his photographic memory. Yet it spoke to me also of myself. Though I had created myself in earlier years in his image, I was now a different person, with different memory treasures. Nevertheless I was pleased to give him brotherly support and found myself happy to be tramping along with him.

Soon I felt another difference in us. Although older than I, he was in better physical shape. He was a runner; he would race along each morning with a stop watch to see what his performance might have gained from the previous day's. I walked only when I needed to—on my way to the commuter train and to my office in the heart of Manhattan. And after an hour or so of hiking on trails in the woods, through fields and various paths in the wild, I was pooped—a term we used back then. So we went back to mother's place for mid-morning coffee.

He was only getting started. Generously, he offered to make the rest of the circle—about 270 degrees—alone, and I sheepishly accepted. This time, however, he took with him a small portable cassette tape recorder. He would use this device to "memorize" what he saw, heard, and felt along the way.

Last night, decades later, and years after his death, I played that tape.

By turning the tiny instrument off and on again whenever he had something to say, he left a fascinating record for me of his recall of this and that new field and meadow and farm and how it had changed over the half century since he had come to know the outer limits, the circumference of our village. I realized somewhat sadly that I had never cared to find out the things he had learned and remembered. What I heard was relevant to my boyhood also, of course, but even more interesting to me was how it revealed his character and personality. Breathlessly chatting as he trudged along through fields and wooded paths, he came excitingly alive—calling out his surprise and pleasure to the trees and birds and whistling breezes and rustling corn stalks—and he could hardly wait to get to the next discovery along this nostalgic odyssey.

He talked to the cows he discovered grazing on a hillside and recalled how he had to take milk pail and stool, find our cow, and bring home the precious milk that helped to keep our family alive during the Great Depression. Hearing him, I remembered when that chore became mine as I wore his hand-me-down clothes and inherited his jobs of milking the cow and chopping wood for the kitchen range. I had forgotten how much "follow the leader" there actually had been.

Both of us survived for more years than we had a right to expect. He wrote his story and called it *Survivor: Knute's Wild Story* (Detroit, Harlo Press 1984).

Bob and Bill share memories during Seattle visit

By the late 1990s I knew he wouldn't be a survivor very long. I flew out to the Seattle area to visit him in a nursing home, an institution virtually next door to the Microsoft headquarters in Redmond, where he could get professional care. Alzheimer's disease was causing his mind to waste away. I knew my meeting with him would be difficult, even though I was more or less prepared—if one ever is for that sort of thing. I didn't expect him to recognize me or know me, but I immediately got face-to-face with him and explained that I was his "kid brother" Bob. "Oh," he said with a smile, or the closest he could come to a smile.

When I came into that room, my first glance around wouldn't have told me that the old man, seen from behind, sitting straight and still with a military bearing, with his all white hair cropped close to his head, was my brother, "Wild Bill," Knute the Survivor, a.k.a. "Ace." He had gained weight. He couldn't run anymore, of course. In fact, he couldn't walk any more.

The Alzheimer's wing of that nursing home was pleasant, neat and clean. I sat with him and helped him as he ate his lunch, feeding him now and then when his attention wandered away from the food. I held his hand often and, when he was awake, he grasped it with an "I won't let go" iron grip. I showed him family pictures. I sang to him, and, at one point, when I was singing from the old black Lutheran Hymnary we had as children in Minnesota, he picked up on the rhythm and clapped loudly to my singing.

His total dependence was a metaphor for his own theology of grace. He would always proclaim that we can't work our way into heaven, but our ultimate salvation was God's gift of grace. I could love him and thank him and pray with him and josh with him and hug him—and all of it was a gift, not so much for him, but a gift for me. I didn't know when again I might see him, if ever. I doubt if my visit helped him at all, or that it was even apprehended. But it certainly helped me. It gave me a sense of peace.

His death came a few months later in the final year of the twentieth century—his century.

Bob and Bill. Brothers. While I may have added some footnotes to his career, he helped significantly to script important chapters of my life, and I thank him for that. As kid brother and big brother, we started our special sibling symbiosis—a fancy term for what it really was: follow the leader.

5 Pacific Odyssey

When I was a child, wars were part fantasy, part fiction, and part history. I was born shortly after the first World War, and I grew up between the first and second wars. Each Memorial Day the veterans in my hometown would dress up in their ill-fitting uniforms and march to our band music out to the cemetery west of the village. Sometimes I was chosen to play taps on a bugle or on my trumpet. The khaki clad men would fire their blanks at the sky.

I remember as a youngster being frightened by some movies and newspaper pictures of the war in China. It seemed the only place on the globe where people were deliberately trying to kill one another. It never occurred to me that I might someday be in the midst of a war.

In January, 1944, I was. It was a time of conflicting emotions. I sat on an ammunition box outside of my tent on the island of Eniwetok and sketched out what was going through my mind.

>What chasms to cross?
>What wild streams to ford?
>What oceans to sail?
>What lands to explore?
>What hours to consume?
>What thoughts to think?
>What dreams to dream?
>What nightmares to fight?
>What reality to face?
>What prayers to pray
>'Til we return?
>
>Duty? Yes! Adventure? Yes!
>*Who knows what to call it?*
>It is life, unprecedented,
>Rich, full—and joyfully so;
>But it is life painfully sad

And painfully lonely;
And it is likewise death.
Glorious? Yes! Noble? Yes!
Who knows what to call it?

It is death cloaked
In all the bitterness of death;
But more—
It is death, hard and nasty,
Gory, ugly, a bad dream
With copious embellishments;
And it is a lonely death.

What work there?
What toil here?
What plans to plan?
What tasks to do?
What hope?
What faith?
What consecration?
What names to honor?
What songs to sing?
What reality to face?
What prayers to pray
'Til we return?

With considerable naiveté I had followed the crowd of my age group into the military. I had registered for the draft, but I wanted to finish college first. My graduation from Luther College was scheduled for five months after Pearl Harbor Day. Following my brother's pattern, I would become a Naval aviator.

Not that I had any particular love for flying. At that time I had been in the air only twice in my twenty years. But I did get a big kick out of my first solo hops. In a light aircraft I learned aerobatic tricks—loops, rolls, immelmanns, spins, and what not.

Learning to fly became a pivotal life experience. I charted new courses for long distance flights, learned aircraft recognition and Morse code, learned to fly by night, and fly blind by instruments alone. Feeling confident in flying depends on how much trust you have in your instruments and in your colleagues. *Keep your eyes open. Look around. Be aware.* Those warnings have stayed with me ever since.

The military system swallowed me, chewed me up by the book, shaped and molded me into something I had never dreamed I would be—a fighting man. It was a heady life begun at the Minneapolis and then at the Corpus Christi Naval Air Stations.

But first the Navy decided, probably because there were more recruits in the pipeline than the NAS facilities then could handle, that they needed to get us in physical shape. So our physical training months were spent on the University of Iowa campus, within which we were aboard what I called U.S.S. *Iowa City*, ironically the most land-locked setting the Navy could find! We lived in a dormitory but we had chow and bunks and decks and ladders and heads and port and starboard and fore and aft so we wouldn't any longer sound like civilians. A modest simulation of life at sea.

My memories of those pre-flight and flight-school months of preparation as a Naval cadet before obtaining my commission are nearly all positive. As sifted through the years, my recall is warm and pleasant and benign. I must have avoided any trauma from the fears and frights. Of course, military discipline itself created pressure to do the right thing. The dreaded penalty that could follow some major goof—or even having three or four down-checks on one's record—was washing out of the program. Perhaps the most difficult were these Iowa months of toughening up under the newly commissioned jocks from college and professional sports whose task it was to build us up physically to meet the enemy. But, strangely, for one who was more aesthetic than athletic, gaining a tiny bit of prowess in boxing, wrestling, swimming, track, gymnastics, and even football and soccer became satisfying. I enjoyed most my discovery and experience with the trampoline. Lt. Hartley Price, our head gymnastics instructor, was quoted in the *Chicago Sun* (2-7-1943) "Trampoline ... It teaches in five minutes what takes years to accomplish—split-second orientation in mid-air—and orientation in the air is one of the basic requirements for a good pilot."

In spite of my rosy memory, the record speaks otherwise. In a card written to my mother during that marathon physical exercise period, I sent her this complaint:

> This day was really rugged! We had a sand-bag test this morning and had to carry one-third of our weight (60 lbs.) on our back and step up and down onto a bench for five minutes in marching tempo. In swimming we had to disrobe in water, inflate our pants and shirt as

life preservers, and float. We had a 10-mile hike this a.m. also, intermittently running and walking. Add to that an hour and a half of gymnastics. I am quite weary, but getting in shape at last, I think.

By the time we entered the war zone in the Pacific, I was already out of shape.

During my flight training in Corpus Christi I was introduced to another phenomenon of World War II that proved supportive to me and many other military souls lifted out from society into a new order of living. This was the Lutheran Service Center, a religious version of the USO concept of serving sailors and soldiers. Pastor A. B. Swan and his wife were host and hostess, and the center was like a home away from home, where I headed when I went on liberty to the otherwise dull town of Corpus. One day Swan invited me to go fishing with him out on the Gulf. I had never done that before, nor did I ever do it again. Later I visited other such centers our church had established—San Diego, for example, and San Francisco.

I also found that my cadet training gave me some (more) confidence in leadership. I was picked as our battalion's lieutenant. Amazingly, this gave me authority over all the other cadets in our bat, although I remained just a cadet through it all. There were perks. I spent time in the battalion headquarters (I was a good typist) and conducted morning inspections of the barracks, even if my own quarters may have been guilty of an unmade bunk and scattered clothing. I stood out in front of the assembled trainees each morning, barking orders for marching, standing at attention or at ease, parading, saluting, or whatever. I never had a moment of stage fright.

That kind of faux glory was short-lived. Yet all through the Navy experience, I felt that I could be comfortable talking with officers above me, both as buddies and as a respectful underling. Through it all I discovered there is something of a trick in relating to authority that involves communicating respect for the other without demeaning one's own self-respect.

I emerged from the other end of training sessions in Iowa, Minnesota, Texas, and California as an officer, commissioned by the President of the United States (via the Secretary of the Navy) as a Naval aviator. Here I was, Ensign Robert Edward Alexander Lee. The Navy demanded that I use all my names—at least it separated me from the other nineteen Ensign Robert Lees in the Navy at that time. But, of course, it was all by the numbers, anyway. You might forget your name but had better not forget your serial number. Let's see ... Oh, yes! 315400.

I wasn't shipped out to the war zones right away. My orders were to report to San Diego NAS at Coronado Island across the bay from San Diego. My new friend Charles (Chuck) Nelson had arrived two weeks earlier from Corpus also with his newly pinned wings. From Michigan, he was Swedish American and a Lutheran like me. We went overseas together and returned together. He is still my best friend.

Bob and Chuck Nelson in 1943 on eve of departure for war in Pacific

We were assigned to the Operational Training Unit (OTU) to spend several months getting trained to fly a huge four engine seaplane called the Coronado. I experienced for the first time the "rank-hath-its-privileges" life as a Navy officer: the Bachelor Officers' Quarters, Officer's Mess (gourmet meals and exotic tropical fruits), and the Officers' Club. We could have massages any time and could enjoy the elegant items in the ship's store.

Soon I was in the cockpit flying the Coronado in Patrol Bombing Squadron VPB-13, located in Hawaii at Kaneohe NAS on Oahu. I was one of four pilots, including the patrol plane commander and first officer. I started as fourth and then third officer and then second, but never made PPC before the war ended. We lower rank ensigns were relief pilots on long missions and usually took turns navigating each excursion over the ocean. As wars go, ours was mercifully short. And I found it fairly safe and antiseptic compared to others' horrendous life and death encounters.

If course it didn't feel very safe when we were bombing an enemy island and were inviting anti-aircraft to shoot back at us, as if we were flying into fireworks on the fourth of July. And it didn't feel safe when we were strafing and bombing a Japanese cargo ship whose guns were firing red-hot bullets our way. And it didn't feel safe as we were flying close to Japan at night with a bogie plane (our "friend or foe" apparatus indicated it was foe!) tracking us off to our right side (pardon me, our "starboard" side). And it didn't feel safe when one day we had a Kamikaze guest at chow time. Our ship—a seaplane tender—was hit. But it would have been catastrophic if an alert gunner had not shot the intruder before he hit our deck. Even so, the explosion nearly knocked us off our wardroom chairs. We rushed out to see the smoldering ruins of the plane and the shredded and strewn bloody body parts of its suicide pilot.

Nor did it feel safe at Okinawa when a General Quarters alarm in the middle of the night rudely awakened all personnel in the fleet in the Kerama Retto anchorage. They then dashed to their posts to send ack-ack heavenward to discourage the Kamikaze human missiles. Suddenly the sky full of bursting pyrotechnic barrages. We pilots had been trying to sleep to prepare for our twelve-hour patrol the next day over the Pacific waters near Japan and China. Since we had no battle stations aboard our host ship, we just stood out on deck gaping at the noisy, frightening Sound and Light show. I found myself shivering in the tropical night.

There was plenty of time in between day-long or night-long flight patrols to muse about our return and what our encounters would demand of us before that time—if God allowed us to survive.

Coronado seaplane with four pilots and crew of fourteen

Near the end of the war our squadron was equipped with a then-new navigation system called Loran. We could find our exact longitude and latitude with the help of an electronic device that could measure the time lag in microseconds between our location and one or two of the transmitter stations that sent out continuous beeps at a predetermined tempo. This was the forerunner of much more sophisticated navigational gear that would follow our war.

One time before Loran, we were virtually lost at sea, and I was grateful that in training I had learned how to use an octant to get lines of position on our map from the stars. On a flight returning from a harried patrol up close to the Japanese Islands, we weren't hitting the visual check points we should be seeing. We didn't take it too seriously until we realized that we weren't spotting any of our expected critical landmarks. I was in the co-pilot seat in the cockpit, and Norm Olson suggested I go back and check with the pilot whose turn it was to do the navigating. I soon discovered from his chart that he was all mixed up and was trying to convince me that all was okay and we were on target. I got out the seldom used octant and climbed up into the dome to get some star shots, noting the Greenwich Mean hours, minutes, and seconds in each case. Then I plotted on our map three lines of position, adjusting for time elapse between each one and advancing the two earlier ones by airspeed calculations. I lucked out and surprised myself by getting, just when I needed it, a perfect three-line fix. The good news was that now we knew exactly where we were. The bad news was that we were about 150 miles off course. We had just enough fuel to make a course correction and arrive at our Okinawa lagoon a bit late, but relieved.

The poor navigator. He seems to have temporarily gone off his rocker. We realized that he had survived a bad episode some weeks before when he was flying with another crew and a takeoff had to be aborted. Normally that's no problem over water. But in this case, Jato bottles—small supplementary lift devices with primitive jet propulsion—had already been ignited, and so, even though the pilot had killed the engines, those Jato bottles still tried to propel the plane into the air. They couldn't provide enough power, so the huge plane stalled at a low altitude, dove right into the water, and sank. Both episodes had had a traumatic effect on him, and after our incident he was referred to a medic for help.

After some sixty years the details get a bit fuzzy. But I have my letters written then and saved for me by Elaine and my family. Our P-boat squadron, VPB-13, has continued to have reunions over the years and recently published a book (*Squadron 13 and the Big Flying Boats*, Hellgate Press, 2005) to which I contributed three chapters of stories.

Those letters were life-savers. Mail call, whether on board a ship or in a tent or billet on shore, was a much awaited event. And precious. Some had no one—friend, family, wife, or sweetheart—to connect with. I pitied them even while prizing my good fortune.

I treasure a Christmas card sent to me by an old woman from my home community, Martha Otterness. She knew me because she was one of my dad's few cousins. She had come from the same Aurland Fjord area in Norway where my Lee (a.k.a. Lie) ancestors had come from. She was a regular listener to my college radio program, *Hymns We Love*, and I had dedicated some songs to her. Her Christmas card had been scrawled painstakingly with only this address: "Ensign Robert Lee, Sam Digo, Calefornia"—no other address (not even her own return address). It was postmarked December 14, 1943, and it reached me in mid-April 1944 with forwarding marks all over it from Camp Kearney, CA, Fleet Airwings 14, 2, 8, Com Air So Pac, stamped "No record Personnel Office Hdqtrs. 11th Naval District." Finally, someone, somewhere had found me in VP-13, and the tiny signed greeting with Christmas candles and poinsettia came, miraculously, to me. I still cherish the message she penned in her shaky handwriting:

> i miss you so much Robert may God bles and take
> car of you that is my Praer for you

In comparison with ground infantry forces inching up Mount Suribachi on Iwo Jima and fighter pilots with their aerial dog-fights and hazardous carrier landings and take-offs, we had the best of the war, if there is such a thing.

But some of us did not survive. Two of my roommates lost their lives. Roland Johnson died with his crew of thirteen when his plane crashed into an island mountain. Cecil Hensel, who had stood next to me in chapel receiving sacramental communion the previous Sunday, perished with all but three of his crew when their returning plane could not land in our anchorage. It had been deliberately fogged in to protect the flotilla of ships and seaplanes from those persistent Kamikaze marauders. Cecil's plane crashed as it was forced to make a blind open-sea landing in the dark of night. His body washed up on the shore several days later. Three of us pilots joined the ship's chaplain as we buried him on an atoll near Okinawa in that summer of 1945. The chaplain suggested we sing the Navy Hymn. Some of us knew the tune, and others just knew the words.

> Eternal Father, strong to save,
> Whose arm has bound the restless wave,
> Who bade the mighty ocean deep
> Its own appointed limits keep:
> Oh hear us when we cry to Thee
> For those in peril on the sea.

Each of us tossed some sandy soil into the grave. I felt the pain of losing a friend.

We searched the ocean for submarines, enemy shipping, and bogeys (enemy aircraft). Our patrols were often routine. Our Coronado had bunks so we pilots could rest between our turn at the controls. We even had a galley, complete with stove, oven, and sink. On these ten- to fourteen-hour flights one of our crew served as chef, which meant that we could have a hot meal in mid-Pacific.

One of our missions was especially memorable. The fleet with its multitude of warships had assembled in an anchorage at Ulithi atoll prior to the expected invasion of Japan. VPB-13 had relocated all its planes and personnel there from Saipan. It was our base of operations for the entire month of March 1945.

During those few weeks at Ulithi, we were able, amazingly, to gather a dozen or so Luther College men from various ships in the fleet for a beer party on Mogmog island (a.k.a. Mwagmwog) on the north end of the big atoll. Somehow a chaplain (I remember his name was Pastor Tolo) on one of the ships put it all together. I remember our singing "To Luther let us sing a joyous song of love and cheer!" It was almost like a visit home.

One day during that month our crew was assigned to plot the location and track the course of a newly discovered typhoon out in the western Pacific between Ulithi and the Philippines. To find the eye of the storm that was threatening Leyte Gulf, we had to fly right into the typhoon, which a pilot in his right mind would never do without a direct order. We had to dive down almost to sea level to track the position and direction of the cyclonic phenomenon that could do so much damage. We had to check the barometric pressure from the altimeter, determine the wind direction by sight, and estimate the storm's speed from the size of the white caps we could see right under our wings. We saw and felt the wash of the angry waves on our aircraft as we radioed this information back to the fleet. When we reached the eye of the typhoon, we actually discovered that the sun was shining there and reflecting its light back from the whitish cyclonic wall surrounding the central core. But it didn't last. We had to re-enter the wicked wind on the other side of the calm.

One day, returning to Okinawa from a patrol near Japan, our plane again started reacting to the turbulence of an oncoming typhoon. It's not the sound that bothers you, it's the shaking. In the cockpit Patrol Plane Commander Norm Olson and I struggled to keep the plane in level flight. Even though the Coronado was heavy, the angry wind tossed us up and down. We gave the order for the whole crew to secure themselves. We approached the harbor as the sun was going down for the day—not that it gave us much light with all the gloom and rain and wind. We couldn't see our landing destination, then suddenly we were right over it. I looked around and wondered, "Where is everyone?" Our squadron and all the ships had disappeared.

After we made a precarious landing, we discovered that all our planes had flown down to Tanapag Harbor at Saipan. Our orders were to get re-fueled and follow them down. Although we had already been out for about twelve hours, to escape the approaching typhoon we faced another long flight of fifteen hundred nautical miles that night. That wasn't so bad, as we could take turns at the controls and we pilots could nap (as if we could in that turbulent weather).

But first we faced the challenge of getting fuel into the plane while we were secured to the fuel barge. Both the barge and the plane were bobbing fiercely on the water, doing a dance to that same "Stormy Weather" music. Those seamen who were the crew of the fuel barge deserve a medal for their heroism. The next challenge was to take off, with those huge swells and crashing surf facing us as a wicked obstacle. Norm and I had all we could do to maneuver the mammoth aircraft's controls once we had turned on full power. We bounced into the air prematurely and, without sufficient airspeed, fell back into the water for another try. We tried again and again, but each bounce increased our vulnerability. If we didn't gain enough airspeed because we were heavier than usual with all that additional petrol, we could easily go into a stall and spin down into the drink. It was dark, and we couldn't see any skyline as reference. We worked hard and prayed hard, and finally the aircraft shuddered and held its place, having gained enough airspeed to stay aloft. We gradually climbed to altitude through the wind and the rain and terrible turbulence. It was one of those situations where we really had no choice but to go full speed ahead.

Another time we weren't scheduled to fly, and we were on board the ship where we lived, our seaplane tender, the U.S.S. *Kenneth Whiting*, when its captain decided to ride out the storm at sea rather than be anchored in the harbor. You haven't lived until you have been aboard a ship during a storm of typhoon/hurricane strength. Some sought refuge in the comfort of their bunks. Others of us wanted to be in the wardroom. The bow of the huge ship lifted up so that furniture and dishes and anything not tied down—including the passengers—slid to one side. When it came crashing down, everything slipped back to the other side.

My memories have their happy side. When not flying we read books and listened to music. One of our squadron pilots was Pegues Kelly, a café pianist from New York, who had at least on one occasion been Judy Garland's accompanist. He and I would find a piano far below deck and sing and play pop songs of the thirties and forties.

I remember doing guard duty after midnight up on the wing of our Coronado that was tethered to a buoy in the harbor. How strange for me to sit with a lethal weapon in my arms to fend off a swimming enemy saboteur while listening to Bach's "Bist du bei mir" floating up from the airplane's radio gear tuned to Armed Forces Radio.

On Eniwetok and Kwajalein atolls we basked on the beaches and swam in the warm Pacific. But that could be dangerous, too. One day I was swimming with my buddy Chuck. He almost didn't make it when he swam out beyond the safety line. The undertow swept him farther and farther away. I was closer to shore and had the dilemma: how to help him? Was there a line, some rope, or any kind of float I could toss him? Finally the sea decided it would lift him up in a huge wave that hurled him back toward the shore where I could grab him.

In Hawaii on its windward side we had the pleasure of living in Termite Village, a collection of town houses that could accommodate about four pilots each. We had separate bedrooms, and there were baths and a kitchen and living room. Chuck was a good cook; we relished his gourmet meals. And because we lived on the Kaneohe Naval Air Station, we could take a daredevil ride in a jitney bus across the Pale—a precipitous mountain road that was at that time almost more frightening than the war itself. But that treacherous route took us to Honolulu, and that was as close to civilization as we could come.

The memories Chuck and I share are most certainly sacred. We joined VPB-13 at the same time and, though flying in separate crews, we were otherwise constantly together. Chuck was younger than I, but he had received his wings about two weeks before I did from Corpus Christi NAS in Texas, and so he technically outranked me. We became like brothers. He was in my wedding party during the war when I married Elaine, and I was in his wedding right after the war in Michigan when he married Barbara. It was both fitting and poignant that I went to his side in Texas when his Barbara died in the year 2000, and later the same year when my Elaine died he came to my side in New York.

I shall never forget the honor Chuck paid me when, after Hiroshima and Nagasaki suffered the atom bomb and the war was virtually over, he was due to return to the States before me with his crew. Instead, he told me he wanted to wait for me, though it meant an extra delay of several weeks for him.

We were there at the big divide between the old and new age of militarism. We were there at the birth of the atomic age. On a regular patrol a short time later, my crew tried to find the city of Nagasaki. It was gone. To us it seemed as if it had never been there! Some of us thought that the *fear of frying*—to put it crudely—in a nuclear disaster would hold all nations in check. Apparently not. The technological world has introduced amazing innovations, and I neither recognize nor fathom most of the incredible devices in use today. Despite the so-called modernization, wars have followed wars. Fighting forces on both sides are following orders—as we did—and are still spreading destruction and chaos and death, not only to combatants, but to innocent civilians. When will we ever learn?

In our war, we as flyers seldom met the enemy face to face. Death normally meant that someone just didn't return from a flight, and we or his family might never know what happened. But I have a vivid memory of one confrontation with war deaths. We flew into the lagoon of an atoll formerly held by the Japanese. The ground fighting had just been completed when we arrived. After getting settled in our tents, Chuck and I decided to inspect the territory nearby, a charred and still-smoldering battleground. The fighting had wasted this island's beauty. We passed among blackened palm trees bereft of their lovely branches. We realized no one had raked the sand. It was dirty with the detritus of war. We breathed the stink of rotten flesh as we walked. We stumbled upon human bodies—enemy corpses still resting in death where they had fallen.

Here was a Japanese soldier. In his pocket peeking out was a letter, probably from home. Nearby we found a Shinto prayer book, a tiny black book the size of my pocket New Testament. In all of wartime carnage, those few fallen soldiers lying in the sand on that Pacific atoll did not count for much beyond the body count. But I wondered how I would feel if one of those who once was a living human being was my neighbor. My friend. My brother.

6 I Sang for My Father

My earliest memory of my dad was when I was a very young toddler. Our whole family had joined with aunts, uncles, and cousins for an old-fashioned picnic. I don't recall that we ever experienced a second event like that. But this one was down by a lively country stream in Minnesota's Yucatan valley, just twenty minutes from home. It offered us a swimming hole. Lots of food. Tablecloths spread on the grass. Baskets of goodies dispensed in potluck style. A glorious occasion!

Some went swimming. I guess I was too small to be in the water but not too small to watch in wonder. And that is when I saw the sight I have remembered all my life: there was Papa—he had donned coveralls, of all things, a most amazing type of swim wear. I remember him dashing by our blanket and leaping into the river! I never saw him swimming again. But then and there he imbued his son with a sudden, surprising spectacle; to me he became an instant hero!

I have to say it was out of character for him to be so demonstrative. His persona was distinctively low-key, calm and collected. He was known for being warm, pleasant, humorous, charming. My brother described him as "laid back." Everybody liked Knute Lee—his seven children, especially. We were taught and trained by our mother, Mathilda, whom we respected with some awe. But we felt loved by our father! That was enough. Our rather assertive and take-charge mother was the family disciplinarian, and good and fair and effective she was, too. When we asked Dad for permission to do this or that, he would often say, "Ask your mother!" But he would slip us ice-cream nickels without her knowing.

Mother now and then would send me on an errand to pick up some last minute item at one of the stores. She simply said, "Get the money from your father." One time when I was a mere six-year-old dispatched on such an assignment, I visited his usual haunts in the village without success, and then on the street I met our minister, Pastor Alfred Johnson. He found it funny and fascinating to hear this little tyke ask him, "Have you seen Knute?" The laughter still resonates embarrassingly in my memory at the retelling of this story over the years. I guess no kid would normally dare to call his father by his first name in those days.

Knute was a friend of almost everyone in our hometown. His office in the K. Lee Feed Barn was a gathering place for his closest friends. The coffee was always hot on the stove, and the room—with its couch and extra chair—usually reeked of cigar smoke. There were signs for DeLaval Cream Separators he sold and several months worth of calendar art on the walls, even including some scantily clothed bathing beauties.

While our mother seldom, if ever, went near the barn, we kids used to enjoy playing there among the hay stacks, horse stalls, farm equipment, and leftover buggies from the pre-war era. Once brother Bill discovered a man lying in the hayloft, sleeping off a drunk.

Julie told me that she and Margaret were even allowed to play in the old hearse that was kept there for dad to collect bodies from among the many deaths during the terrible 1918 Spanish Flu pandemic. When someone died, he would hitch up a team to go out to some farm and bring in the deceased—usually someone he knew.

His closest friend and neighbor, Johnny Kjome, was stricken by the dread disease. Dad sat with him for hours the night he died and finally came home to report the tragic news to our family. I am sure he wore a mask then; during that crisis children even wore masks when they went to school each day.

Dad had beautiful curly hair and kept it neat with frequent visits to one of his barber friends. Unlike most of us men today, he had a barber-chair shave almost every day.

He was an active participant in local affairs—a volunteer fire fighter and a member of the school board. He was elected constable, but his duties were mostly limited to serving court papers on delinquent tax payers or mortgage holders. And a couple of times he put himself on the county ballot to see if he could be elected sheriff. He never got elected. But I think he enjoyed the campaign process. He took me along as he drove an old truck around to farmers and chatted with them and gave them his card with his picture on it. I remember that he sometimes left his lighted cigar in the ashtray of the truck while he left me in the cab and walked up to the house or the barn to solicit votes. A couple of times, I recall, I snatched a few drags from the smoldering stogie—awful stuff, I discovered. Although for too many years I was addicted to cigarettes, I never smoked cigars later in life. Dad was hardly ever seen without his cigar. I still think of him when I catch the aroma of that pungent smoke.

Dad's schooling was limited to six grades. When he grew up in the "gay nineties" there was no high school in our town of Spring Grove, Minnesota.

Young men of the village or the nearby farms were neither encouraged nor expected to continue their education, although a few valiant souls found their way to an academy that led to college—and some from our area even followed it by graduate work toward becoming a minister or doctor. Dad never mentioned his limited schooling, but instead insisted that his kids have a good education. And in spite of the Depression's economic disasters, they all completed higher education, some going on to advanced degrees. His service on the local public school board confirmed his ardent support of schooling.

One cultural gift he did learn in his limited schooling was an appreciation for poetry. In those days, pupils had to memorize poems on a regular basis. My mother and my older sisters would always clean out pockets before doing the laundry, and there in Dad's overalls they would discover clippings of poetry; for example, verses of Edgar Guest. "The Poet of the People" was syndicated in several hundred daily papers, including, no doubt, the *Winona Republican Herald* that came to our house every day. Guest's homespun lines connected with average Americans like my father.

Knute had an artistic bent. His handwriting was beautiful—carefully cursive, with a flair for a gently curving script. He wasn't observed reading very often, and when he did read, it was likely something in Norwegian, the language of his childhood. A Norwegian newspaper came to our house regularly in the mail; both our mother and father must have felt that their "mother tongue" spoke most clearly to them. On Sundays, while the rest of us attended the English language service, Dad usually went alone to the later service in the Norwegian language, an option that prevailed for most of his life in our ethnic enclave. We used to joke that in Spring Grove even the dogs barked in Norwegian! But after World War I, during which the Germans were our enemy and foreign languages were often suspect, English gradually overwhelmed the Norwegian that for many in our community had for years been the language of the heart.

My father didn't live long enough to grow old. He died at sixty in 1939. I was in college. Strange how memory fades and yet lingers in wisps of emotional recall. I had only seventeen years with him. I can "see" him, but not too clearly. The pictures of him as a young man, especially as a bridegroom, reveal a very handsome fellow with a thick thatch of black hair and a rather strongly chiseled face. His deeply set eyes and heavy eyebrows gave him a look of distinction. He looked out at his world with warmth. People felt that; his children, especially, felt that. Later his dentures (upper and lower) seemed to change his countenance and give his mouth a downturn. I always also felt his smile hid a trace of sadness. Perhaps it was because he was never fully fulfilled.

Dad was a dreamer, I think, and he was born to the wrong century. History was against him. He was trapped by a limited education. He had built his vocation on a mode of transportation that was swept into cruel obsolescence by the automobile.

My brother Bill and I talked together about that one day over coffee in the kitchen of the home in the Seattle area where he and Shirley lived. We agreed that the world of twentieth century progress passed him by. Bill put it this way:

> He was engrossed in his work with the horses. At that time, in the early twenties, horses were instruments of toil and labor before automobiles and tractors ever came into general existence. And so he worked with horses. He was a horseman. He never really shifted into the gears of the automotive world. He sort of staggered around with them. He didn't know cars, but he knew horses!

He had bet on horses as a staple of farming and transportation. Early in our parents' marriage, he and our uncle Arthur had taken the train out to Montana and bought a carload of wild horses that had been captured. He brought them back to our town and "broke" them, as they then called the domesticating of the steeds, training them and selling them to farmers who needed work horses to pull wagons or sleighs or plows or buggies. He himself had teams of horses he hitched to a carriage; he was one of our community's first rural mail carriers. At Christmas time his fans along the route would leave bags of grain by their mail boxes for him to feed his teams.

Dad also had a business of operating a feed barn in the village—a kind of horse hotel. Farmers brought their teams to his barn where he fed them, curried and cleaned them if necessary, while their owners did their "trading"— selling eggs and milk and cream and other home-grown produce in return for the flour, sugar, coffee, and canned goods they needed.

Everyone in Spring Grove and environs knew that Knute Lee had a full measure of horse sense. It was an event in our family when the horse traders came to town. As a child, I never knew or understood just what the odds were, but I sensed from the snatches of adult conversation that it was Papa's game to see if he could outwit the touring traders of horseflesh. My brother would let me share his fantasy about the perfect pony that one day would occupy a stall in the barn. We had even selected a name for "our" mount. But it never came. Another work horse would always take up residence in the stall we had reserved our own hoped-for animal.

I actually was given a horse one time, I have been told. I was much too small to ride it alone. But I have a picture of myself at age two or three sitting in front of my father on that horse. Her name, I think, was Cora. Bill remembered the words I proudly spoke to my family when Dad and I rode up to show off my horse: "When I'm small I hold one strap but when I'm big I'll hold two straps!" In spite of that impetus and inspiration, I never became a "two strap" horseman.

Little Robert riding with father

I find it fascinating that none of Knute's children ever had an affinity for horses, but several of his grandchildren do. My daughter Sigrid takes riding lessons near her home in Italy and at this writing has two horses to feed and care for and—I hold my breath—ride.

As a special treat our father would draw a picture for us of a horse on the kitchen blackboard. It was a perfect picture, tenderly chalked for us with artistic grace, and it would remain there unmolested for weeks. As far as I know, he never drew anything but that horse. But with that exquisite talent, he might have been an artist.

His children didn't see as much of him as we wished because he was busy with his horses and feed barn and farm machinery and dray line. (A similar lament my six kids may have had about me!) He came home for dinner at noon, took his nap on the dining room floor, and absented himself until supper time. After supper, I am sure to the disappointment of our mother, he would usually meet his friends around a card table in the back of some restaurant in the village. When he came home late, Dad would always check on every room to be sure that his children were safely tucked in. Sometimes we would hear him come but pretend to be asleep. Recalling this ritual is a comforting memory.

Our father was musical. He loved to sing. And we would sing as a family, with sister Julie playing familiar tunes in any key we wanted. "Play 'Roses of Picardy,'" he would ask Juliet when she went to the piano. And he would sing or hum along. Another favorite also in the wake of the war was "Over There." I remember his singing with me "In the Shade of the Old Apple Tree." When I hear one of those tunes these days—even silently hearing it in my head—I think of my dad.

He had a fiddle, although we never heard him perform. In the early years of their marriage, he had an accordion—he called it a "squeeze box"—and people remember hearing him on summer nights when the windows were open. I know he appreciated the music his children added to the atmosphere of our home: singing, piano, and, for Bill and me, trumpet playing.

For a while, our father made a decent living for his family in those years before and after the First World War. Up until the Great Depression. That's when his businesses all began to fail. Poor Dad! He was not an efficient manager. He had a sign on the door of his office in his huge feed barn in the alley behind Main Street: Cash or Note. The note was simply an I.O.U. signed to confirm that the buyer of twine or hay or milking machine or cream separators would pay later. During the Depression many never paid, and Dad held these worthless notes. He was too easy-going to pursue the debtors. Or he may have just been a realist, as he himself likely had more bills on hand than he could pay. It was a rough time. I am sure it was an emotional struggle and a source of much anxiety for my parents.

Yet I don't remember that it was a sad or morose or downbeat time. At least we kids growing up in that desperate time seem to have been shielded from the ogre of poverty and deprivation. We never went hungry. To be sure, our menus were simple and, at least for the many mouths around our table, were seemingly adequate. Our mother had studied and taught nutrition and made sure that the essentials for health were on our table. We had a huge garden, and we kids had to hoe and weed and harvest its products.

In his last years Dad wasn't well, and our mother wrote us of his struggle to walk to his job as manager of the local village-run liquor store. He didn't like that work, writing to one of us that each night he had to "fight with drunkards and half wits!" But his modest salary helped us survive.

If he had lived in today's world he might have added another fifteen or twenty years to his sixty. But he had a bad heart, made worse by his addiction to cigar smoking—he finally quit just ten months before he died from a heart attack. We know he had a premonition of death. Just two weeks before the end, he wrote this to my brother Bill:

> I am feeling fairly well. I still have spells, mostly in the morning. This morning it was at 5 o'clock. I tried to get up (as usual) so Ma doesn't hear me. And when I am quiet about 10 minutes, it is mostly over with. Still, I think some day it will get me!

Remember the movie *I Never Sang For My Father*? I gave the actor Melvyn Douglas an award on an ABC-TV broadcast on behalf of the National Council of Churches. But I *did* sing for my father. Not just casually around the house but one special time. It was the day he died.

At the time, I was at Luther College in nearby Decorah. I remember that he drove me down to school that fall, the one and only time he had done that. It's a precious memory. But about six weeks later he happened to be listening to me on the radio program broadcast over KWLC, the college station. I was singing hymns, as I did each day. He was at his work and the radio was on, as it was every day. I was told by one of his last customers that he had my voice filling the shop. Less than an hour later, he had a severe heart attack and died.

The consolation of that memory will live with me until I die.

7 Academic Discoveries

While I was grateful, I was also embarrassed when the President of Susquehanna University in Pennsylvania read the generous citation from the stage of a crowded auditorium, and several important looking faculty draped me with an honorary hood. I was being awarded the degree of Doctor of Fine Arts.

Fine, indeed! Of course I knew exactly what it was—an honor given in appreciation for my film productions, principally, I gathered, for *The Joy of Bach*. I worked for the Lutheran Church at large and mingled daily with colleagues addressed Doctor this and Doctor that. It didn't matter, apparently, in our setting, whether the doctorate was academically earned or not. I tried to pass the word, at least within my staff, that I did not want to be called Dr. Lee. But other colleagues didn't get the message.

I was surprised one day a few years ago when my barber, of all people, called me Dr. Lee. He was an immigrant from Uzbekistan who became an American citizen. How did he know, for heaven's sake? So I asked him; he said my own pastor had been in for a haircut the other day, and they had talked about me. That's what he had called me, so Boris figured he should also.

Over my career I had taken graduate courses at the University of Minnesota and New York University, but they were for professional training rather than for qualifying for an advanced degree. Before I graduated from Luther College, I lusted after graduate study, but it was not to be. The war came, and I attended the U.S. Navy's so-called University of the Air. After I had been flying over the Pacific for a couple of years, the A-Bomb suddenly ended the war for us, and I was liberated. But I needed a job and began a career that never seemed to lend itself to taking time out for an advanced degree.

I learned that I didn't need it.

I was nevertheless called upon to lecture at colleges and seminaries, teach at an academy for radio announcers, and teach for three semesters at Adelphi College. Despite having only a B.A., I felt comfortable in all those roles.

The G.I. Bill was one of the most creative and catalytic acts our U.S. Congress had ever attempted. It meant that we veterans returning from both Pacific and European theaters of war could get a new start with a college education or an advanced degree. I couldn't drop everything to take full advantage of it because I had a job in radio, just where I wanted to be, and I needed to support my wife and daughter Peggy, the first of our six kids. In 1946, a stimulating opportunity to teach budding radio announcers was dropped in my lap. The Brown Broadcast Academy in Minneapolis asked me to teach evening classes. I had never heard of it, but one of my fellow announcers had worked at the Academy. Someone must have heard me on the air and liked what he heard. I discovered that I had an intuitive talent for helping would-be readers of news and commercials make their vocal communication more effective. As is often true, I probably learned more from teaching others than they learned from me.

The post-war world was ripe for a media and technology explosion. Still in its infancy, television was just beginning to appear in places like New York, L.A., and Chicago. I began to hear about the new academic and commercial field that suddenly became widely known as public relations. At the University of Minnesota School of Journalism I found a course that probably changed my life. At its foundation was the idea that institutions could not take their customers and the public for granted. We heard the classic example of the Bell System (AT&T in those days) training their employees to realize that they were not in the business of just making money, Wall Street notwithstanding. They were, rather, in the business of helping people communicate with each other. That same perspective of serving rather than exploiting the public was applicable to almost every field.

The University also offered a course I felt I wanted and needed: creative writing. I registered for that next. I learned some basic principles of storytelling that have stayed with me through the billions of words (who's counting?) I have written over the sixty plus years since.

Before beginning the radio series my Lutheran denomination offered me in 1947, I told Dr. J.C.K. Preus, then the head of education for the denomination, that I felt the need of some more training on a professional level. I had learned about a summer program at New York University. Dr. Preus (we called him "Kalla," an affectionate term for him as Elaine's uncle) thought it was an excellent idea. The church would pay for the program, including my travel expenses to New York and the cost of living in Manhattan for a couple of months. Of course I missed being with Elaine and baby Peggy as much as they missed me, but I reveled in a wonderful hands-on experience in writing, directing, and discovering the magic of radio drama. Our teachers were top writers from the networks who invited us to observe some of their live studio productions.

Apart from structured learning, each day was a discovery. I was a news hound and kept up with the world—as a broadcaster I had to. I loved interviewing people and was stimulated to discover so much from that process. My kids would kid me about it: "Oh, oh, here comes dad with his microphone again!" Even without a microphone, I found that I was addicted to asking questions.

As one raised in an environment like mine, I couldn't avoid having intellectual curiosity. At home in Spring Grove, we lived symbolically and literally right next to the large school house. Our house was full of teachers and would-be teachers. Our mother was a teacher in name and in fact.

I always felt that the members of my family were highly intelligent. At least two of my sisters and I had double promotions in grade school. We called it "skipping a grade." My sister Naomi was at the top of her class. My wife was ahead of me in mental agility. And each of my six kids is, in my honest opinion, more intellectually gifted than I am or ever was.

Of course, at home I had learned how to please my teachers! I relished every bit of my eleven years of attending classes in my hometown's public (and only) school. I later came to realize that I got so involved in extra-curricular activities that I neglected formal study patterns. Music, drama, and journalism all contributed more to my career than math or Latin or history or economics. I was kept busy in chorus, band, vocal and brass quartets, solos, operettas, class plays, declamations, and dramatic readings. Of course, I am grateful for the grounding in the basic curriculum as well. In spite of my undisciplined style of study, I got reasonably good grades, except in physical education, agriculture, and shop. But being neither an athlete nor a farmer nor carpenter, I survived.

So when the doors of Luther College opened for me, a penniless Depression kid, as the direct result of the intervention of my big brother Bill, I was truly surprised and overwhelmed. It was a heady trip for this small town kid—I was only sixteen, and it would be several months before I would reach seventeen—to set off for college. A brave new world was opening up.

Suddenly, there I was. In a dormitory room. Mowing campus lawns. Painting walls. Filling out forms. There were only a few of us on campus that summer. I was able to mix with others who were students with jobs or part of the support staff in various college offices that remained open and active in that off season. Somehow the word had been passed along that I was a good typist. The business manager's secretary was off on vacation, and he was seeking a temp to fill in. Could I do it? Sure. No shorthand skills, but I could take dictation on the typewriter. Fine. I was hired to do it. And I pleased Karl Hansen (he was known informally by the students as Tobak) who was in charge of everything related to the business of running a lively institution. Tobak dictated, and I typed as fast as he could talk. I tried to be careful and not make mistakes, so I wouldn't have to retype the letters. And he tried, I know, to be deliberate and not change his word flow in midstream.

Of course for me, office work beat manual labor; I relished the golden opportunity to continue to work in the business office. Then another grand opening was dropped in my lap. Among the clerical tasks assigned to me by Tobak's assistant, Frank Barth, was to match campus work assignments with a list of students qualified for those jobs. I was one of those students, and so I was expected, presumably, to include myself among the assignments. When I looked over the openings, suddenly I saw "Radio Station KWLC." Eureka! I didn't know it then, but I had stumbled on a pivotal link toward a coveted career in broadcasting. Years later, Frank's life and mine would again intersect meaningfully when his son married my daughter. Although that marriage did not survive, we have two grandsons in common.

Doors kept opening for me that summer before my freshman year. Bill had talked to Maestro Carlo A. Sperati, the legendary conductor of the Luther College Concert Band. My brother must have told him about my winning a trumpet playing award, so an audition followed. I brought my horn to Sperati's house and was interviewed by him; he asked me what I wanted to play. I just happened to have with me the solo, "Sounds from the Hudson," that won me the prize. Several years before, when Bill was in the band, I had seen Sperati conduct it with the fabulous baritone player, Helge Nasby, as soloist. Now in his home, the old veteran musician, still sprightly in his eighties, took the music and sat down to his piano to accompany me.

I made the band roster. In fact, I had the rare honor for a first year student (still just sixteen) to perform this piece as soloist with the band at one of its first concerts that fall. And the doors kept opening.

When I became a sophomore, Sperati promoted me to first chair trumpet. That meant that I took most of the solo passages in classical compositions, marched up with other brass players for the final strains of our signature Sousa march, "Stars and Stripes Forever," and supervised the other trumpet players when sectional rehearsals were required.

If I ever had been tempted to "think more highly of myself than I ought," as the Pauline letters in the New Testament put it (and I fear I sometimes did think that way) I was humbled by the young man sitting next to me that year as the second chair player. Bud (Adolph) Herseth was very good indeed. I quickly became aware he was much better as a brass musician than I was. Though I knew—and he knew—that he could play rings around me, he did not qualify for first chair because he was "just a freshman." We became good friends, and our friendship has lasted through many years. For fifty and more of those years, Bud remained as principal trumpet for the Chicago Symphony Orchestra. I have been told that he was one of the world's finest trumpet players. Back at Luther, I soon realized that I was a dilettante, and with all my singing and radio involvement, no one would mind if I slipped out of the concert band in my final two years at Luther. I have hardly picked up the trumpet since—and I haven't missed it.

The faculty person assigned to supervise the radio station was Dr. William Strunk, head of the biology department, who knew little about radio. He sensed that I could figure it out, and he more or less let me to do what I wanted to do. KWLC was in sad shape—it had become almost an afterthought to the campus community. I saw it, however, as a marvelous chance for the college to serve the area public and at the same time communicate the values of the college to an audience that I believed we could multiply. It worked pretty well. I gave all the time I could to announcing and program planning. At homecoming I took a microphone out among the gathered alumni crowds and did "man on the street" interviews with them.

I managed a coup one day—unplanned, to be sure—when the Crown Prince and Princess of Norway were visiting the campus. He was speaking in the C.K. Preus Gymnasium, the largest hall on campus, used for music, stage plays, and various public events. The campus was almost filled with people who had come to see the royal couple, but these visitors couldn't get into the packed gym. I was at the main entrance several steps above the crowd, describing the scene to the radio audience. Suddenly there was commotion inside and the doors opened. Out stepped the Prince and Princess. Here I was, next to them with microphone in hand. Quickly we switched on the public address system, and I boldly announced, "Ladies and gentlemen, His Royal Highness, Crown Prince Olaf of Norway!" Applause! Instinctively I handed him the mike. He took it, and with all the sophisticated confidence that royalty should have, he made some kind remarks to the people who had gathered. The newspapers said that there were about seventeen thousand persons there, more than Decorah or Luther were used to having.

After my first year, when my music making became generally known, I was invited by three upper classmen (a sophomore who was a tenor and banjo virtuoso, and two seniors who sang baritone and bass) to form with them a male quartet and tour the Midwest over the summer months. We called ourselves The Norsemen. We planned several types of programs and memorized all the songs. I was assigned second tenor. In addition, I accompanied the banjo player for his solos and the baritone for his. I was elected to be the speaker for the group and also to play a trumpet solo. That meant I had to secure a local accompanist each time. That was a bit tricky, but I was lucky. Together we bought an old Model A Ford to travel in as we made concert stops in Wisconsin, Minnesota, North Dakota, and Iowa for several months in the summer.

We had an accident with that old Ford one day toward the end of our tour. I was driving at the time on a county road that led from Minnesota into Iowa. We had no collision nor mishap with another vehicle. We were, however, suddenly alarmed at strange sounds coming from the car—not from the engine but from something below like a wheel. Indeed, a wheel! With a loud bang and a crunchy sound, the car shook and seemed to limp along the gravel road. And then we saw it! The front left wheel had broken loose from its axle and was spinning speedily down the road. As we watched in fear and horror, it leaped into the ditch and came to rest against a fence. I somehow was able to bring the Ford safely to rest on the shoulder. How did we ever proceed after that? I have no memory of what happened next, but I am guessing that the upperclassmen took charge when they saw the freshman was too spooked to help solve the problem.

Most of the programs on that tour were in churches. Usually there was a free-will offering to cover our travel expenses, and each of us received a quarter share of what was left. It helped me finance my second year at Luther.

It turned out that, for the most part, I did work my way through college. My brother and sisters, most of whom were teaching and thus salaried, were wonderfully generous, and I have always felt indebted to them for that sacrifice. I did receive some fees for singing at weddings and funerals. One local Lutheran pastor would depend upon me as a talent resource for such ceremonies within his congregation or the community. I substituted some Sundays for my friend Weston Noble, who was organist that year in the Methodist Church in Decorah. One summer, I was hired to direct a county women's chorus. I had never done anything like that but I knew I could do it, and I did. The women seemed to love this young conductor and sang their hearts out for me. We traveled to the Iowa State Fair and won a blue ribbon in our class.

A local radio personality became a good friend of mine, one I respected highly. He was Georg Strandvold, an editor at *Decorah Posten*, the Norwegian language newspaper that over the years had covered the immigrant community in our country. He had come to the U.S. as a journalist from Denmark but wrote Norwegian (a similar written language then) beautifully. Though his English was slightly accented, it was impeccable. I put him on the air each week. He was wise and knowledgeable in interpreting the implications of the hostile international scene. I believed in him and his program so much that I managed to get the larger and much more influential radio station, WMT in Cedar Rapids, to pick up the program for their own listeners. In those days, with more limited long distance routing of programs, at least for poor local stations, we made acetate recordings (large sixteen-inch platters) of each weekly program and sent them by bus to the Cedar Rapids station from which they would be transmitted. It worked.

I was now given complete responsibility for all the programming at KWLC. In auditioning would-be student announcers, I discovered several excellent voices. One was Lyman Peterson, who had a beautiful baritone radio voice—I wonder whatever happened to him—and Jerry Rosholt. I saw Jerry as a talent in many ways. He could act, he could write, he could ad lib, and he was smart. Proof of that, in my view, was that after the war he was hired by Associated Press and ultimately by NBC as the chief writer for the Nightly News Show with Huntley and Brinkley. I myself hired him in 1962 to help me publicize and promote the feature film I had produced, *Question 7*.

At KWLC we produced some modest radio dramas, and we were able to arrange with the Grand Theater in Decorah to broadcast these before a live audience once a week. Oh, yes, we were on a roll.

One of my good friends, among many at Luther, was Elaine Naeseth. She was an excellent pianist and often accompanied me when I was called upon for a vocal solo and for some of my *Hymns We Love* broadcasts as well. She was one of the women students I dated occasionally. I didn't seek out romance, both because I was so involved in my various tasks and because I really couldn't often afford to invite a girl out for a movie or a meal or a snack. But Elaine was the kind of friend who appealed to my soul. She had a wonderful sense of humor. She was smart and clever and loved to write notes and play games. She sang in a trio and in a women's quartet. She sat next to me in a German class and slipped me fractured German messages as we were passing on campus or sent them to me via an intermediary friend. She was fun. She was a year ahead of me, and when she was out teaching on her first job and I was a senior on campus, she returned frequently to visit her sister Margaret, who was our college nurse. That's when we intensified our interest in each other. As they say about Western movies, "Now, cut to the chase!"

The upshot of that is that Elaine was the girl I married. But more of that later.

I guess it is only fair for me to indicate that I did take courses and attend classes also. My favorite subjects, and those that later proved most helpful, were religion, music, and German—in that order. But my life at Luther was fulfilled by the extra-curricular stuff. And while I did minimal study, mostly I bluffed my way through courses, just as I had done in high school. A pity I never really learned to study. But life proved to be my laboratory.

No narrative of my college years in Decorah would be complete without a tribute to my aunt and uncle who lived there. A childless couple grown old, Maria and Charlie Peterson lived in a small cottage near the railroad tracks. In his youth Uncle Charlie had been a rather wild character, I was told. A star baseball player in the local leagues, he had found it difficult to conform to established mores. He had often been discovered in the throes of a drunken stupor. But he had turned seriously to religion in his last years. They loved to have me come and visit them. Aunt Maria would feed me, indeed over-feed me. But I enjoyed having a retreat corner in town where I could just be me, without the trappings of all the collegiate appurtenances. Aunt Maria was my father's only surviving sister, and when he died in 1939 in my second student year, she was devastated. I did my best to comfort her, and my attempts to do that comforted me.

The loss of my father affected me greatly. He was the first of our family to die. I hurried home (after informing Aunt Maria, who took it very hard) and fully immersed myself in his final rites. When I returned to school, I found myself meditating about the loss and reflecting on my father's influence on my life. In my grief, I even wrote a song.

The event of Pearl Harbor on December 7, 1941, shook the world. And it shook me and my classmates and our whole college community. I remember well a group of close friends from the senior class walking together down to a nearby bar and drinking beer at midnight while we ruminated on the implications for us in this tragedy.

What now of my future? I would get my B.A. degree in May, and then what? I kicked around the options with my friends who had similar questions. Would I follow in the path of my brother Bill, already a Navy pilot in the Pacific? Was I flyer material? I didn't feel any kinship with aviation, really. But at least it had some drama and excitement and offered a special challenge. I might try.

Before I could get an appointment for a Navy test and physical examination, I witnessed a local disaster at our college. The venerable Main Building— the precious symbol of Luther College—was destroyed by fire.

I was scheduled to sing some solo roles in a cantata to be presented in the Preus gym/auditorium on that Sunday afternoon in late May. The audience was gathering and the orchestra was tuning up. We were backstage studying our scores when someone burst in to shout, "Main is on fire!" We ran to look out the window, and there was a dark billow of smoke pouring out of the top of our proud, castle-like campus icon. The cantata was instantly forgotten. The room where I was living was in that building. I rushed over and quickly grabbed an armful of books and clothes and whatever was readily available, hauling it down three floors to the back of the burning building. Foolishly, I left everything in a pile some feet away from the structure. Sadly, it was not far enough. All my stuff was ruined, either scorched or soaked by water. Yet I knew that my pain was inconsequential. There was work to be done. All of us who had been drawn to the scene helped salvage valuable papers from the business office and dean's and registrar's offices.

When there didn't seem to be any more we could do but watch from a safe distance on the campus, I remembered who I was. I still had responsibility for KWLC as its main staffer. We were on the air at that time, broadcasting some symphonic music. I ran to the tower studio in the gym to find Oliver Eittreim, the veteran electronic master of the station. He found me a microphone and amplifier and long cord, and I took the extended mike out on the campus and began a play-by-play description of the fire. As I was explaining the critical problem of low water pressure encountered by the firefighters, my fellow announcer Jerry Rosholt appeared. We took turns at the mike. While he continued the descriptive patter, I went out among the gathered crowd to pick out this or that person whom I thought might have a good story about the building, to give a context to its importance and comment on the loss that was being witnessed at the moment. Jerry would pass the mike to me, and he would seek the next person to interview. We knew we had done a first class job of on-the-scene reporting. Apparently it was widely heard; people came to the campus from all over the region to witness the devastation for themselves.

An article in the local newspaper a few days later confirmed:

> Never before in the history of the Luther College radio station were KWLC radio announcers and staff in such top form …
>
> Bob Lee and Jerry Rosholt relayed their microphone directly to the center of the Luther campus for the broadcast.… Despite the tension and nervousness which accompanied the viewing of Old Main's flaming demise, the account of the spectacle was delivered by the announcers who succeeded in painting an accurate picture of what happened …
>
> When sign-off time came, an eloquent picture of Luther's "thumbs up" policy was painted by Bob Lee, in drawing a resemblance between the annual Homecoming illumination of Old Main and the blazing holocaust that gutted the building. It was the final conclusion of the day over KWLC that the towers of Old Main still pointed heavenward, the imperishable traditions of Luther College still dedicated to the Glory of God alone, as in its motto, *Soli Deo Gloria*.

The next day Jerry had written and broadcast a beautiful script as an homage to the landmark building, now a pile of smoking rubble. The entire text was also published by the local newspaper that week.

I left my college experiences there in Decorah among the smoldering ruins of this shrine where I had worshipped and studied and listened and sung and prayed. I departed shortly afterwards for the U.S. Navy. For flight training. For action in the Pacific Ocean, trying to help fight a war.

As I left, I saw a sign that someone—I think it was Professor Pip Qualley, who taught classics—had mounted in front of the ruins. It carried the phrase *RESURGAM*. I was soon to learn what it meant: I SHALL RISE AGAIN.

8 SNISKET

Oh, how I miss her! My wife Elaine. I think of her each day. As I get out of bed each morning, I voice in my heart the prayer to thank God for Elaine.

A part of me is gone. We truly did have a union of our two lives. We merged more than our bodies; it was as if we merged our souls as well. I have wept, mourned, prayed, and remembered. I poured much of this into my book, *Dear Elaine*. That labor of love, plus time itself, have given me God's gift of healing.

But there's more to tell about this amazing woman. Not secrets, although some of those may even escape. More about the profound experience of our marriage, because it remains a basic part of who I am.

She was never "Snisket" to me. Yet I name this chapter after the loving nickname her brother Erling gave her. She didn't mind. This term of endearment reveals the side of Elaine that existed before her name changed from Elaine Naeseth (pronounce it at your peril!) to Elaine Lee. Because this Snisket name wasn't part of my experience with Elaine, it represents to me Elaine as an heiress of the Brandt and Naeseth family legends and legacies. If the Norwegian-American pioneer immigrants ever had a social class close to aristocracy, her forebears must have been included. She had an inherited sense of style, of propriety, of *noblesse oblige* that revealed a hint of royalty. One acquaintance described her as "such an elegant lady!"

Her being raised in a Lutheran parsonage is not just incidental to Elaine's persona. It was not always easy being a "P.K." (preacher's kid). The Naeseth children often felt that they were on a pedestal, that the congregation their father served for all of thirty-five years seemed to feel they owned the family. Or maybe the parents were over-sensitive to the strength of the messages their style of living sent out to the parish, intentionally or otherwise. While young Elaine and her siblings acted their expected roles most of the time, they often found the rituals comical and were tempted to rebel—and sometimes did. But they never (or seldom) were known to embarrass the pastor and his wife.

Churches are notorious for under-paying their clergy, and Elaine grew up during the Great Depression, as I did. Being poor was not a shame in those days. And the good Lutheran congregants of Spring Prairie, Wisconsin, saw that the pastor's family had food and clothing. Elaine told of finding eggs and generous cuts of meat contributed by farmers and baked goodies from the farmers' wives. At Christmas time, especially, there was always a goose or a turkey left anonymously on the back porch.

The parsonage children were grounded in faith. They were expected to become role models, mirroring a spiritual force inculcated into each of their lives almost automatically—as a natural course of events, a given. Like many of us they spent years sorting out the personal meaning in all the absorbed doctrine, ritual, and mystery of the religion bequeathed from pious parents. Elaine opted for spirituality notwithstanding the doctrinaire pressures of her religious upbringing.

Elaine was born in Valley City, North Dakota, while her father, always called C.G. (for Carelius Gunnarson), was pastor of a Lutheran church in that town. She was just an infant when they moved to Wisconsin to serve the two-church country parish where the Norwegian branch of the Lutheran church in America had its beginning in 1847. The congregation had pride in that. Spring Prairie wasn't just any rural church at a county highway intersection.

Her dad was rather rough-cut for a pastor. He wasn't cheerfully voluble, as many spiritual shepherds are supposed to be. He was thoughtful and deliberate. His austere and erect presence could be intimidating. His sense of humor—wry and dry—was often hidden, but when revealed, could be warm and tender under the veneer of the public role he felt he had to play. He was seldom without his pipe.

Her mother, Emma, was cozy, always smiling (in public), and a faithful and competent but not brilliant musician. Elaine emulated her in many ways but exceeded her mother in demonstrating bold and dramatic vivacity in music and in personal relationships. Whereas C.G. reflected farm life, Emma came from what might be called an aristocratic clergy family, the Brandts. Elaine's Uncle Walther was a history professor at City College in New York, and her aunt, Diderikke (always called Dikka) was married to a Preus, from the top tier of Norwegian American Lutheranism's unofficial class structure. Dikka's husband Kalla had once been a parsonage child and grandchild at the very Spring Prairie home where Elaine spent her youth. And Kalla's brother had been governor of Minnesota. The Naeseth side had famous relatives also: Eric Sevareid, the late CBS star reporter and war correspondent, and I must include a famous cousin (third or fourth?) back in Norway—the former Sonja Haraldsen, now the Queen, wife of King Harald.

By the time I arrived at Luther College in the fall of 1938, Elaine was already in her second year. We connected in a most oblique fashion, and for most of our years together as students we were friends—good friends—but little more than that. She was fun. Her humor was entertaining. Her music was delightful. She had a way at the keyboard, whether piano or organ, that made the instrument sing. She seemed to express her personality through her music—playing and singing and improvising and, now and then, composing. Most of her friends, naturally, were fellow musicians. I could observe her from the sidelines and realized that college people, both faculty and fellow students, were captivated by her flair, her friendly and cozy joshing with them.

I might have been emboldened to date her, but it was well known that she had a steady boyfriend, Perry Dungey. I knew him mainly as a bassoon player in the Concert Band. I never warmed to him, and if you can read between the lines, it is not difficult to figure out why.

Elaine sang in a trio of college women as well as in a quartet. I put them on the air over KWLC even in my freshman year, when we would broadcast programs of music direct from the small music building (affectionately called the "Chicken Coop") that housed faculty teaching studios and practice rooms with pianos or organs. Later on she accompanied me for my weekend *Hymns We Love* broadcast.

About the only time she got into trouble, as far as I know, it was mostly my fault. We had a date of sorts and went out to the Green Parrot Tea Room for sundaes or sodas. We were so engrossed in our chatter about mutual interests that I brought her home after the strict curfew at her dormitory, and she was "campused"—confined to the academic area as a mild punishment—for two weeks. I even went to plead my guilt to the dean of women, but to no avail. Clara Paulson played no favorites, even though I knew she was fond of both Elaine and me. Of course, no one sentenced *me* to any limitation! In those days women students were to be protected in a special version of *in loco parentis*. It had been only a few years since Luther had adopted co-education.

Elaine was seen as special by some faculty members, especially those in music. We were in a German class together. Dr. Wilhelm (Billy) Sihler was our professor—a charming import from Europe with a sense of humor expressed with a twinkle, a wink and a smile, and often outrageous sarcasm. He made learning German fun for us. Dr. Billy offered her a special advanced German class alone for credit. His only stipulation was that after the tutoring session, she accompany him on the piano as he played the cello. Elaine was the perfect accompanist for his fine playing.

She similarly got along comfortably with Dr. Theodore Hoelty-Nickel, a top musician and an aspiring musicologist—he had studied in Leipzig, Bach's hometown. Elaine did some baby sitting for Nickel and his wife. He had recognized Elaine's talents from her first days in his class. Both of us took a conducting course from him. That was a riot: he didn't bother much with the technique of conducting but taught us about scores and had us follow them as we listened to classical recordings supplied to the college by the Carnegie Foundation.

And the piano-organ teacher, Professor Donald Larsen, knew all about Elaine. He came from the same parish in McFarland, Wisconsin, where Elaine's grandparents lived and had their ministry for years. Larsen was organist for our wedding.

It was mainly after she graduated that I realized she cared for me. As everyone who knew her can attest, Elaine loved to write letters. And she enjoyed writing to me because, as a correspondent, I sent replies back quickly and gave her back sassy, smart-ass slogans sometimes worth a laugh. That paid off for both of us when I joined the Navy soon after my graduation in 1942. She wanted very much to stay in touch with me, and our romance blossomed by mail between us two separated lovers. It's a different way to get intimately acquainted, but my saved letters show we were able to share a lot of ideas during that time. This process helped each of us to get a depth perspective on the other. We revealed our convictions, our moral and ethical standards, the many facets of our Christian faith, and we could play games with each other—word games or puzzles. She would send me telegrams in verse or sometimes encrypted so I would have to struggle to figure them out.

On May 8, 1943, Elaine had traveled from her teaching position in Janesville, Wisconsin, to where I was at the Twin City Naval Air Station at Wold Chamberlain airport. One of her classmates, Stella Barstad, was married to Luther graduate Ensign Arnold Temte, a friend of mine who taught math to us cadets, and Elaine was their guest for that memorable weekend. We had enjoyed a delightful dinner at the Curtis Hotel (it no longer stands, alas!) in spite of her having a painful toothache. Perhaps a little wine at dinner helped. We repaired to a balcony on the second floor that overlooked the cityscape lighted up for the evening. Something told me, "This is the time to pop the question." Something told her to say yes almost instantly. Of course we could not set any date, because my future was in the hands of the U.S. Navy.

What does one say when caught up in the glorious epiphany of such a profoundly sacred moment? Seldom am I found to be at such a loss for words. My heart told me to sing: on the way back to the Temtes' house in a taxi, I crooned some love songs, including the war-bond winning "As Time Goes By."

When I told my mother that Elaine and I were engaged and would be married, she said, "Aren't you a little young?" I didn't argue with her. At that time I didn't know that my mother actually was my age (twenty-two) when she and Dad got married. Brother Bill also had cautioned me to go slow with romance. From his duty station on the coast of Oregon, he wrote me at the Minneapolis Naval Air Station:

> So you're in love with Elaine! Well, I'm glad you chose a nice Christian girl. But these times are not too ideal for falling in love, although there is no control over that. Do you contemplate marriage soon? You had better wait until the war is over. Don't you think so? Of course I don't know what you are thinking or what your plans are, but I don't suppose you mind my remarks.

I was soon to go out to fly for the Navy in the Pacific, but midway through the war, in the summer of 1944, our squadron was given a month of home leave. Elaine and I took advantage of it to schedule our wedding at Spring Prairie. Her quartet colleagues from Luther came to make up the bride's attendants, with her sister Louise as maid of honor and her cousin Lois Brandt as a fourth bridesmaid. And, miraculously, Bill was also on leave and was my best man. (He had graciously come to respect my decision not to wait until the end of the war.) My Navy buddy Chuck Nelson and my sister Margaret's husband Paul Thies were my attendants as ushers.

I was honored my Aunt Maria was willing to come. This was the only time I had seen her away from Decorah or Spring Grove. Although travel wasn't easy in that war-time period, all my sisters were there except Naomi, who was with her husband stationed in Nevada. Chuck, his mother Louise, and his fiancée Barbara Winters had crossed Lake Michigan from their home in Muskegon. I was gratified to have him there and pleased to meet his mother and his fiancée. Bill, Chuck and I looked elegant in our dress whites, and Paul blended well in his white suit.

The family and wedding party had gathered on the parsonage lawn, less than a half mile from the church. Then everybody left for the church, and Bill and I were alone in the parsonage. Whether it was our bantering or arguing or just a case of nerves, we lost track of the time and arrived over at the church ten minutes late. To my own wedding! At the altar while reciting vows before the still stern Pastor C.G., about to be my father-in-law, my knees were being just slightly exercised with a gentle shaking.

In 1944 the Spring Prairie Church was an active congregation of mostly farmers. A good core of these locals attended the reception in the church parlors, as they called the basement space below the sanctuary. They laughed with us at brother Bill's words, as people always do when he is in his entertainment mode. My Decorah friend Norman Bradish, retired philosophy professor, offered a sophisticated toast—with punch rather than alcohol, I am sure.

The quartet, including the bride in her white gown, performed at the reception. Everyone laughed when they belted out a close harmony pop tune of that period, "Can This Be Love?" The bride and groom performed as well, the bride improvising a delightful accompaniment to our duets. For the occasion I had written a love song: "Whenever you need me, I'll come at your call. Whenever you need me, ask for anything at all!"

Elaine's dad offered us his car for the honeymoon weekend in Chicago, leaving himself with no car. What a gift that was. We stayed at the Ambassador Hotel and had dinner in the Pump Room of the Palmer House. We also heard the Chicago Symphony at Ravinia. The lively Offenbach operetta tune "Gaîté Parisienne" fit our ebullient mood.

A few days after our return to Spring Prairie, C.G. took us to Portage to catch the Hiawatha for LaCrosse on the Mississippi. Bill met us, and we drove the thirty miles to our mother's home in Spring Grove. It was a rare experience to "cuddle" with my wife in my own upstairs bedroom. It was good to have this additional time with Mother and some of my sisters, and especially to get caught up on our respective war experiences (the uncensored version). Mother must have been wondering about what was going on in the Pacific with her sons.

Elaine and I had only a few months to live together out in San Diego before I shipped out again to fight the war some more. Thus began our married life that was to continue for more than five decades. Our life in the Quonset hut in San Diego was a special time for us as man and wife. While we had known each other for almost five years before the wedding, we realized that we didn't really *know* each other until we lived together. I have often thought of how good it was that we waited until we were legally and spiritually wed before consummating the union in the full sense of giving ourselves sexually to each other. To many young people today, it seems that such waiting is unnecessary and pointless, but to us it was precious. And for Elaine, who is famous in our family for delayed gratification, it was the perfect way to maximize the gratification that sexual intimacy offers. I remember so well in Chicago on our honeymoon almost singing to myself—or maybe aloud to both of us—"This is IT! It is right. It is good. It is perfect, as it should be!"

Some may be surprised to learn that, in spite of our six children, we did practice contraception. But we also coveted children, and God gave them to us as a marvelous and blessed gift. The timing was managed by both of us in agreement. I have to laugh a bit as I recall Elaine's needing to seek out a gynecologist while we lived in San Diego. We had discovered that the Navy had that kind of medic in addition to other specialists. The kicker is his advice to Elaine that, because of a tipped uterus, she might never be able to bear children. We sure fooled him.

I am so proud of Elaine as a mother. I only have to look around at our family to realize that the way they turned out to be such humane and smart and loving human beings is largely to her credit. I know that. And our kids know it too.

I live with some guilt pangs for having been an absent father so often. My job had demands that included considerable travel. As a result, this husband and father wasn't home to help wife and mother. My whole career included a mobility requirement, and though sometimes Elaine could join me in Germany, in Norway, in Paris, or at the Cannes Film Festival, most often she had to bear the burden of parenthood by herself.

The logistics of her traveling with me included her making arrangements for our kids, especially when they were young. When our nest emptied, of course, Elaine found it much easier to join me—at least to the extent that our bank account would allow.

It was good that she enjoyed playing with numbers and taking charge of the family accounts. We were on one salary most of the time, and the fact that the church does not pay market-place compensation meant that we had to scrimp and scrounge to pay our bills on time. More than once, we had to get bailed out with a bank loan. Both of us hated doing that—the albatross effect—but it solved the immediate problem at the time.

Elaine was able to take some freelance music gigs. A number of schools in Baldwin and in our Nassau County area discovered that she was a good accompanist for school concerts and musicals and operettas. She was good at that and was in demand. Similarly, she did stints as church organist, often at our Bethlehem Lutheran church in Baldwin—even at one time for a couple of years. She also enjoyed substituting on a weekly basis and had calls from a variety of congregations. In church, Elaine had a refined sense of timing. At the organ she anticipated each part of the service and could effect modulations—from one mood or key to another—that were always creatively seamless. She also found fulfillment in being on the worship panel for the Metro area Lutherans. Hymnody became a special interest for Elaine. She had grown up with hymns—she knew hundreds by memory—and could play them straight or ornament them and build improvised chorale preludes on them as needed.

One of her great musical joys was working as the musical director of the radio program we began in 1947 for our Lutheran Church. I was in charge of Lutheran Sunday School at Home by Mail and Radio. Together we conceptualized and produced *Children's Chapel,* a quarter-hour weekly program of dramatized Bible stories with hymns and prayers. We reached a vast audience of kids over about two hundred stations. Elaine composed all the background and mood music, as well as bridges for the drama for several hundred programs.

Elaine improvised musical transitions for radio drama

We lived in Great Falls, Montana. Our second child, Barbara, was born while we were there. Our first, Peggy, born in St. Paul during my time at WMIN, was less than two at the time. When we discovered that we could not produce the radio series effectively from Montana, we had to travel every few months to Minneapolis, where studio facilities allowed us to realize first class programs. It meant that we traveled from Montana by Pullman car on the Great Northern Railroad—the Empire Builder. We had a compartment room, with seats facing each other for daytime travel that became bunks for us and the children overnight. At our hotel in Minneapolis, a dresser drawer became Barbara's crib. Also, we had to plan our production process around Elaine's need to breastfeed Barbara.

We often had a good laugh when we recalled her once composing a song based on a psalm for the shepherd David to sing, writing it while she was in the bathroom at our hotel. She dashed it off, and we included it in the drama we recorded that very afternoon. Elaine made the music sound suitably pastoral and Hebraic.

Elaine built lasting friendships with many of our neighbors and friends in the various places we lived. In Richfield, a suburb of Minneapolis, we joined Woodlake Lutheran Church and became friends with many families there. Elaine and her neighbor Birdie across the alley got together each morning for coffee. After both moved elsewhere in the country, they kept in touch and enjoyed many letters and occasional visits.

We lived in a small house in Richfield. Our four children at that time—Peg, Barbara, Sigrid, and Richard—were all still small, and we had no trouble fitting everyone in. But it was good we found a somewhat larger house in New York where we moved next—and where we remained for a half century—so we could have bedroom space for two more who were born as native New Yorkers, Sylvia and Paul.

In Baldwin, New York, our main social connection was through Bethlehem Lutheran Church. It was there that Elaine discovered Mary Knuth. They were like sisters and understood and supported each other. When Mary was struck down with cancer, Elaine (with the rest of our family) participated at a special healing service—our first.

When I was drafted to be a liberal candidate for the local school board, the campaign included meetings—kaffeeklatsches—in many homes. Usually Elaine went with me. Most of the families were Jewish. I found they supported education more solidly than did my Protestant compatriots. In this process we discovered many new, wonderful friends. I would join many of them on my daily commute into New York City on the Long Island Railroad.

It was important in Elaine's life that she not abandon her music potential. On her own she located an excellent and seasoned piano teacher, Alexander Lipsky. Many of our albums of Bach piano works in our house had his name on them as translator of the notes. It turned out that he was in the pedagogical lineage of teachers leading back to Beethoven. Elaine loved her sessions at his home studio in Manhattan, and she usually enjoyed being on her own in the city. We especially remember one incident at Lincoln Center. When she stopped to check on a musical score at the library there, she was mugged as she got off the subway. A gang of teenagers grabbed her purse and ran with it. She lost all her money, of course, but a policeman lent her enough to make a call to my office from a pay phone so I could come and rescue her. She was terrified by the assault, but did not allow it to interfere with her lessons. It helped that, weeks later, someone who had found her driver's license and some of her credit cards strewn on Broadway mailed them back to her.

She was conflicted when she took on a long-term job as an organist: she felt that the keyboard touch—and the pedals connection—were different enough so that she should really be studying organ instead of piano. Thus she enrolled as a part-time student in organ at the Westminster Choir College in Princeton, where daughter Barbara and her husband Eric lived. So trips to New Jersey for lessons meant seeing them also. One time she stayed there for several weeks, living in their apartment while they were on vacation.

Just as Elaine's childhood in a Lutheran parsonage was formative, so also was her relationship with her four siblings. Her sister Louise lived with her husband Fred Hubbard in many places on the globe, including Paris, Edinburgh, Manila, Honolulu, Sri Lanka, and even Nepal. As a water resources expert, Fred was a busy consultant for the United Nations and individual countries that were trying to update their basic infrastructures. While they were living in Washington D.C., Louise and Fred provided a recovery retreat for Elaine during a particularly stressful time. The Hubbards took it upon themselves to provide Elaine with their own version of a health spa. And it worked. They even took her along camping to the Blue Ridge Mountains of Virginia, a new experience for Elaine.

Elaine and Louise had bonded firmly in their childhood. Both had gone to Luther College, both had been teachers. When we were young parents, Louise had come to help us out with a new baby. And when Louise and Fred moved permanently to Hastings-on-Hudson, just a fifty-minute drive from Baldwin, the sisters could talk on the phone often and visit each other frequently.

Elaine saw less of her other siblings. Snisket was close to Erling, though. He and his wife Sally and their family lived in Decorah. We spent several summer vacations with them. They generously welcomed our family to their house on Center Street, right across the street from my brother Bill and his wife Shirley and their kids. (Both Erling and Bill were on the Luther College faculty at the time.) The children found the Decorah swimming pool just down the block a great attraction each morning, giving the adults time to "visit."

Elaine's sister Margaret was farther away, in Alaska with her husband, missionary pastor Norval Hegland, and their three children. Later they lived in the West, in Washington and Oregon, South Dakota, and even Kansas. Partly because they saw each other so seldom, Elaine and Margaret hadn't bonded quite as firmly as had Elaine and Louise.

Elaine's older brother, Gerhard (Gerry), was a scholar—a librarian, as was his similarly intellectual wife, Milma. He was a pioneer in Norwegian genealogy, recognized for his research—in fact he was knighted by King Olaf of Norway. Elaine and I admired Gerry's concentration on his work, but had few opportunities for personal contact with him.

Although Midwesterners, Elaine and I spent most of our years on the East Coast. We lived in a suburban community very near the south shore of Long Island, where we were a family of "beach bums." The famous Jones Beach was just a few miles away, and in the good old summer time, Elaine would load up the car—when the kids were young, we wore out both a Ford and a Chevrolet station wagon—and pack lunches and drinks and towels. In about twenty minutes we would be there to spend the day on the sand and in the water. Paul remembers his mother's artful sand castles. She always had a book at hand, as well as pencils and paper for puzzles. It was the good life.

Later the two of us sought out winter vacations in sunny places. We planned frugal vacations: on our trips to the Caribbean we even packed staples and frozen food in our checked baggage. We loved the freedom of being practically alone on the beach on the small non-touristy island of St. Eustacius.

When we decided to splurge a bit more, we chose St. Martin, the French half of the colonial island shared between the Dutch and the French governments. For a couple of weeks we rented a small but cozy studio apartment in a duplex a short walk from the beach. We loved the accommodations at that quiet resort. It was there that we met Marla and Al, strangers from Cape Cod who suddenly became dear friends. They spent several months there each winter in their own little cabin. Elaine and Marla discovered they had the same loves: beach, books, culture, music, games, and, especially, letter writing. From the first days they felt a soul-sharing relationship, developing a sisterly connection that blossomed beautifully by mail. (My book *Dear Elaine* is packed with their letters.) For two women who only met in person two or three times in their life, their sudden and growing symbiosis of personalities and passions had to be more than mere coincidence. They kept in touch for some fifteen years until the end of Elaine's life. Thank you, Marla Crawford, for the gift to Elaine of your friendship.

Elaine had much going for her. We always saw her as an obvious winner. Everyone who knew her did. But, strangely and sadly, she didn't see herself that way. Mothering six children may not have left her with the energy to envision herself other than as a homemaker. When the children no longer needed her on a full-time basis, she grasped for self-confidence and couldn't find it. Although I tried (maybe too hard), I couldn't find it for her. She needed to feel that she was capable, important, loving, useful, and significant. She had all those traits. But something psychological seemed to prevent her realizing that goal. What was it? Was it something I did or did not do? Was she intimidated by my confidence?

I wondered if she was suffering from a clinical depression. We found some answers when, in the 1980s, we were trying to find out why she had a troublesome and persistent cough. She sought diagnoses from various specialists and underwent the usual tests, scans and all.

I thought of something that could lead us to a solution. My employer, the Lutheran Council, offered psychological help to its staff people and their families. We had free access to these professional consultants, who helped families work with issues they didn't otherwise know how to solve or resolve. Though I had previously advised my staff to use this resource, I had never allowed myself to feel that I or my family needed such help.

We explored that route. Both of us were invited to a session where we were interviewed by a psychologist, first together and then separately. Our purpose was to see if the cough might be psychosomatic, as some medics along the way had suggested. Elaine was referred from those sessions to a counselor close to home on Long Island.

And he did help her. But not in the way we expected. After a number of sessions, he came up with a surprising diagnosis for her. He felt her symptoms fit, of all things, alcoholism. All of us in our family, I think, and any others who knew her well, found that hard to believe. Usually an alcoholic is the last to admit that he or she is addicted. Surprisingly, Elaine found she could accept that verdict readily. She had actually suspected it, she said, when she realized that more and more, she would reach for the bottle of wine for calming her troubled soul and quieting her unwanted anxieties. Even I had teased her sometimes about being testy when she drank wine, especially red wine. But Elaine, an alcoholic? No way!

But none of us argued that with her or even tried to disabuse her of that judgment. She quickly joined a support group—she had researched AA herself years before when one of her close relatives had symptoms of alcohol addiction. She entered a group and announced to them boldly: "My name is Elaine, and I am an alcoholic." She kept this up for almost fifteen years, and she claimed it saved her life. She remained faithful in attending AA meetings, sometimes every night in the week and some mornings as well.

Meanwhile, she became disenchanted with the counselor who had rendered this verdict. A family friend who was herself a psychologist recommended a North Shore psychiatrist. Elaine sought him out, and he helped her with her disease, which he diagnosed as a mild depression. Later his psychotherapy was combined with pharmaceutical help.

These nostrums like Prozac worked and didn't work. She lived with the knowledge that the current good feeling could—and likely would—wear off. And the dear doctor, stymied by the vagaries of her case, tried one prescription after another. Usually there was a time period needed after stopping one medication, and then another period of time before a new drug would take effect. This often left Elaine on an emotional see-saw and even, it seemed, a rollercoaster.

The vicissitudes of Elaine's health failed to prepare me for the next phase. I was alerted by a phone call at the American Bible Society in Manhattan. She wasn't very coherent in telling me what was wrong, but this itself was a serious new symptom. She had become dizzy walking to the library a few blocks away. She couldn't keep her balance, and her speech was slurred. Having had no prior experience with strokes, I suggested she call her psychiatrist to find out if the new medication he had prescribed could be causing the difficulties. And then I rushed for a train to take me home.

The next day in the hospital, a neurologist announced that she had suffered a mild stroke. The word "stroke" sent shivers up and down my spine. But the doc was right. It did turn out to be mild. Even so, we had mobilized the family. The children sent messages and rallied to their mom. After a few days in the hospital she started physical therapy, and we started feeling more hopeful.

We pleadingly asked the neurologist if she could make the trip to Iowa for our planned Golden Wedding Anniversary party to which we had invited a hundred guests. "By all means go and enjoy it!" was his welcome advice.

We had planned ambitiously. We all traveled to Decorah, and on the Luther campus where Elaine and I had first met (and where two of our six had been graduated), we hosted a weekend for our relatives and friends. It allowed us to mix with loved ones from various stages of our marriage. We exchanged greetings and memories, took pictures by the dozens, watched a video slide show highlighting decades of family life, sang at a special songfest, and worshipped with our own clan. We included in the service a memorial for Elaine's brother Gerry who had died the previous month. I still see the happy face of Elaine, not yet fully recovered from her first stroke, speaking to the crowd and telling them how much she loved all of them, how she loved me, and most of all, how she loved God! I have watched it again and again on the videotape.

The other public event of note was our celebration of Elaine's eightieth birthday. We had a party at home in Baldwin, and friends and family dropped in for brief chats with her. At the time (only a year and a half before she died), she was suffering from yet another stroke—limited in speech but clear in mind. She had difficulty holding her head up as she sat in her wheelchair. And she could no longer smile—her trade mark was finally denied her. Perhaps the birthday party was more for us, her family and her friends, than for her. Knowing Elaine's proud nature, I realize that she was uncomfortable as so many of her loved ones came into our home to see her as she really was. She wasn't the Elaine they knew, and she knew it.

Her last years, she battled mental deterioration from several progressively worse strokes and hospitalizations. In the late 1990s she also fell and broke her hip, further aggravating her mobility. Times were most certainly difficult for her. But also for me.

It is therapeutic for me to rehearse and recall how this became a beautiful and fulfilling period of my life. I firmly believe that being Elaine's caregiver, especially near the end, was the most noble calling of my career. I knew full well that she was slipping away from me, from us. But I didn't want to surrender. Nor did she. We did talk about life and death. As she shared her fears, she also shared her faith. We would pray together. We would read our favorite scripture.

Toward the end when she had difficulty speaking, she would still follow each word. Often, when I would pause as if to wait in recalling the next word or phrase, she would automatically supply it—faintly but clearly. Even that evidence of her still-alert mental response was a gift to me. And it might also have been reassuring to her. When we said good night, I would pronounce the familiar benediction we had been hearing all our lives:

> The Lord bless you and keep you.
> The Lord make his face shine upon you and be gracious to you.
> The Lord look upon you with favor and give you …

"Peace," Elaine would whisper. I came to understand the rich depth of that word as an emotional and spiritual blessing.

I thank God that Elaine's humanity ended in a merciful closure. She breathed her last while hearing the words of prayer. When our moment comes, might we all have a blessing like that.

9 Faith-based Life

My religious journey began long before I became aware of it. Yes, I have a certificate that verifies that I was baptized as a child in my local Lutheran congregation in Spring Grove, Minnesota. There was only one church in our town of about eight hundred souls. There is a historical reason for that: the immigrants in the mid-nineteenth century were almost all from Norway. Norway was officially Lutheran, and my hometown followed that tradition.

That experience of exclusivity was both good and bad. We knew that our way of believing and worshipping was the right way. I concluded, as I think we were supposed to, that thus everyone else who believed otherwise was wrong. Many sects and denominations also claim that, whether explicitly or implicitly. I felt I had graduated out of the ghetto when I came to realize that we were not the only ones who had the right way and whose faith required respect and acceptance. How else could we live with our Roman Catholic, Orthodox, Jewish, Muslim, Hindu, or Shinto friends or acquaintances, as well as those with no religion?

Lord, I believe. Help Thou my unbelief!

I have called forth that biblical quote repeatedly over the years as I have pondered the mystery of faith. It summarizes the ambivalence that I feel as a life-long Christian. In the face of so many scientific discoveries and developments—not least the creationism vs. evolution debate—how can one be absolute in one's convictions? On the one hand, I accept by faith—not logic or science—the promises of Scripture that have been reinforced by experience, tradition, and the trusted testimony of "a great cloud of witnesses." On the other, I also respect the unbelievers who depend upon rational explanations.

I live by the principle that my faith is not something I chanced upon or swallowed gullibly or earned, but something that comes as a gift from God. How? I don't understand how. But I have been helped by my mentor Martin Luther, who wrote in his sixteenth century catechism, "I believe that I cannot of my own reason or strength believe, but that the Holy Spirit has called me by the Gospel and enlightened me with his gifts …"

Faith has made a marked difference in my life.

It means that I feel on filial terms with the Lord of All Creation! I am comfortable waking up in the morning and, sitting on the edge of my bed, uttering a prayer of thanksgiving for "a new day of grace." And at night, I love to fall asleep in the midst of a "thank you" prayer. It is that gratitude that undergirds my living. This is no exclusive secret, but for me it unlocks some of the overall motivation that facing the new day requires. It helps to calm my anxieties—I am as vulnerable to fear as anyone in this volatile and dangerous time, and I have to intentionally try to avoid negative directions waiting to claim my psyche.

Having emerged from an absolutist religious conviction, I am dismayed that the Christian faith I treasure has been used to manipulate political ends. I am sad that the Christian-flavored political right wing has contributed to the tragic polarization here in the United States. While I am gratified when one of our political leaders shares his or her convictions sincerely, I resent any attempt to gain votes with that technique. The politicization of religion or the evangelizing of politics is wrong, at least in my opinion, and harmful to both the church and state. Theocracy does not have a good track record.

Back in Spring Grove, not only did we have church school on Sundays, but we had "released time" religion classes during school hours. Minnesota had a law that permitted religious training if neither controlled nor mandated by the state. That meant that we pupils were dismissed from our building, and we repaired to a small separate structure for an hour a day of biblical study and indoctrination. I have come to appreciate the grounding in faith and religious information those hours gave me.

Perhaps if I had gone directly from my strict orientation into the secular world, I would have had warped opinions about the belief systems of our nation and the world. But college—even a church-related school like Luther—helped me to have an open mind, a need and desire to search for knowledge and to stretch my preconceptions on most issues, including religion. And then, following those formative years of doctrinal exposure, I was thrust into World War II.

The war put most of my beliefs to the test. I found my faith terribly important as I was sent off as a Navy flyer to the Pacific theater of that ugly war. Being with such a heterogeneous population in that time, I came to appreciate ecumenism and interfaith mingling. I also struggled with issues of death and life and killing and hating the enemy and the awful sentence of those suffering from war wounds—all these had a spiritual relevance for me. I valued chaplains and their service. While I shuddered at some of their sermons, I enjoyed bull sessions with them about theological questions and their relevance to who we were and where we were.

I remember how reassuring Psalm verses were to me as I voiced them while waiting in a line for the runway before takeoff. What better time and place for this passage from Psalm 121:

> The Lord will keep you from all evil; he will keep your life. The Lord will keep your going out and your coming in from this time on and forevermore.

Overseas I found these lines from Psalm 139 so helpful:

> Suppose I had wings like the dawning day and flew across the ocean.
> Even then your powerful arm would guide and protect me.

And in the midst of all this personal drama, I found myself in love, engaged and, halfway through the war, getting married to my dear Elaine. This was factored into my spiritual biography as well. After all, the mystery of love is a spiritual force that we can only partially understand. It is not something that we can set up as a goal and achieve by ourselves. Like other spiritual gifts of faith and hope, love comes to us without design. This happened to me, to us. Some might say it is simply the human process at work, but I will always believe that this gift came through the spirit of God, breathed into me. I was a changed person as a result of the marriage. Suddenly I wasn't living for myself, I was living for us.

After the war, my work required considerable air travel. As a veteran Navy pilot, I assumed I would be at ease flying in a commercial airliner. But I discovered I was experiencing a strange kind of anxiety. I thought it was probably part of a psychological withdrawal from my routine business of flying in wartime, an activity now spilling over into civilian life. Part of the problem, I came to understand, was that I was not in control. With instruments in the cockpit to look at, we as pilots were always informed about altitude, airspeed, climbs, and rate of ascent and descent. But when I was back in a passenger seat every change of sound in the engine would make me wonder, "What's happening now?"

I experienced a bit of panic twice in bad storms. One was on Northwest Airlines flying in Montana in a thunderstorm at night. The pilot was flying low in a valley and, as I looked out the windows in the coach section, I could see the mountains to our right and left, especially when the lightning illuminated the landscape around us. Another time was flying Air France to Mexico City. The storm then was bad, too, and I am embarrassed to remember I was frightened.

I found I just wasn't trusting the pilots. (They hadn't been trained by the U.S. Navy!) In both instances I found myself recalling the New Testament account of Jesus with his disciples crossing the big lake in Galilee during a severe storm. Jesus was asleep in the stern of the boat, and the disciples were terrified as the boat was taking on water from the towering waves. They woke up Jesus and asked, "Teacher, do you not care that we are perishing?" He rebuked the storm, and it calmed down. And Jesus scolded the men, saying, "Why are you afraid? Have you still no faith?"

That rebuke was for me also. It helped me know that the arm of God would guide and protect me. After that I don't think I was ever again fearful while flying, though I have been in a lot of rough turbulence since.

In my air travels there also have been transcendent epiphanies. I sighted the northern lights while flying near Iceland en route to Europe and was awed by the snow-capped peaks of Mont Blanc, Mount McKinley, Fuji, and Kilimanjaro. These were much more than sight-seeing memories; they were spiritual experiences.

Without doubt, the most moving of prayer-filled airborne moments came on a return flight to Manhattan in mid-September 2001. I wrote to my family about it:

> Notwithstanding the hourly television roll of horror images of the towers dissolving into dust and smoke, for me the most haunting picture came as I was looking down from my American Airlines window last night. Finally, I was returning home after frustrating delays in Florida. We had descended into the flight pattern up the Hudson River before making our banking turn down into LaGuardia.
>
> It was a crystal clear night, and Manhattan welcomed us with thousands of lights. The brightest were at the lower tip of the island … and then it was there! But of course it wasn't there. Instead, a haze of rubble dust caught the arc lights, and through that veil we looked down on the ghastly scene where the WTC towers had stood so proudly just days ago. In fact, I had said goodbye to the old Manhattan skyline on Tuesday morning less than 30 minutes before the first attack. We were happily on our way to Tampa, where I expected to be met and taken to the bedside of my sister Margaret in the nursing home where, as an Alzheimer's patient, she was being given tender loving care.
>
> It was 10:10 a.m. that fateful morning when the pilot in a strangely tense voice told us there had been a terrible attack on our

country involving passenger airliners crashing into the World Trade Center towers and into the Pentagon. All aircraft in flight were ordered to land, and we had been ordered to go to Atlanta. The phones were all tied up. I worried about Peg—I knew she had been at the World Trade Center just the night before and worked within a short walking distance from there on Wall Street. It was afternoon before I reached her. She was safe! But meanwhile she was worried about me, knowing that I was aboard an American Airlines flight that morning and that it was an AA plane that was reported to have been the first "airborne missile." After a long wait in Atlanta, I finally settled for a ten-hour bus trip to Florida. Even that part of the journey was blessed for me by an in-depth dialogue about matters of the heart and soul with my seat-mate.

Getting back home was another adventure. Once planes were permitted to fly again and I was finally scheduled out, all flights were cancelled. The next day I discovered from a weary ticket agent that the problem was crews—she softly confessed that they had had crew resignations following the disaster. But she gave me a special gift, too. A first-class seat. And, indeed, the service was first class! For the first time in my air travels, I was the first one off the plane.

For many of us, 9-11 will be a pivotal event within the basket of human and spiritual emotions—sorrow, fear, sympathy, love, hope and, yes, faith.

Faith followed me—or preceded me—in each phase of my career. I started out after World War II on a career of radio broadcasting in the commercial world as an announcer in St. Paul and Minneapolis on WMIN. I was quickly promoted to producer and broadcast executive in programming. After just two and a half years, God claimed me for similar but different service for my church, when I agreed to develop for my national denomination an outreach program by mail and radio to scattered families in the mountains and prairies of America. Along with a correspondence Sunday school for children who lived nowhere near a local parish with a school program, we also created a weekly radio program featuring an on-air devotional time with a dramatized Bible story each week. This is where I came in—I got to use my talents in scripting and producing those stories.

In those days, radio drama was an art form that was very popular with adults and children and served beautifully for those isolated families. Radio drama is almost a lost art in this day of visualized entertainment. But our project was before the television era, before videotape, before DVDs and iPods. I still feel the concept of inviting listeners to "see" the action being played out through their imagination should rank as highly as telling the story with pictures. It puts viewers, young and old, through the exercise of using creative fancy and imaging as a mental process. Have we have lost this precious art?

THE MINNEAPOLIS STAR

MINNEAPOLIS, MINN., TUESDAY, JUNE 8, 1948 ★ 21

MAKING A RECORDING OF ONE OF THE SUNDAY SCHOOL PROGRAMS that will be broadcast over 23 stations is Robert E. Lee (left), director and his cast of actors. They are Paul Borge, station director at Luther college, Decorah, Iowa; Bill Lundquist, Daryl Feldmeir and Dick Stevens, students at St. Olaf college, Northfield, and staff members of station WCAL. The recording was made at the Paul A. Schmitt Music Co.

★ ★ ★ ★ ★ ★

Having made that career change to church broadcasting while still in my twenties, I was enticed to utilize my creative experience and ability even more. After taking a course at the University of Minnesota in public relations, I established a news bureau for our Lutheran church. In that post-war, G.I. Bill era, the big corporations were forming propaganda operations. The church had news too, and I think I helped it to be reported faithfully. Our task was to present the news so that the reporters and editors of daily papers would want it, depend upon it, and use it, if not verbatim, as a basis for their own stories. Our philosophy was to help journalists cover religion more effectively.

At the same time, the commercial world was waking up to the value of visual aids. The church was leaning toward slides and film strips, even productions with recorded sound. I became interested in producing short inspirational 16 mm movies. Paul Rusten, a photographer friend of mine, had talked the church into supporting a unit he ran to produce these shorts. This office came to be known as ELC Films (ELC standing for the Evangelical Lutheran Church, then the name of our denomination). I prepared some scripts for him and helped him produce, edit, and distribute these to audiences, mostly in church basements. I was already continuing the Children's Chapel radio show and supervising the news bureau as assistant director of public relations. After Rusten left, I was asked to direct the film unit. I was juggling quite a few balls in the air.

In the midst of this circus—not to mention my own active domestic life with three and soon four children—the collective group of Lutheran congregations and regional units in America had produced a big movie, *Martin Luther*. It was good enough to be shown in movie theaters. Even before it was shown, it was controversial because of Roman Catholic animosity to the story of the monk Luther who tried to reform that church. The producers came to me in Minneapolis, showed me and other churchmen the completed movie, and asked me to take charge of having the world premiere in our Minnesota area. I was busy enough without that added assignment. I really did not want to do it. But the secretary of the ELC, to whom I reported, felt I should, even if my other work might have to be delegated to others. So I was off and running, with still another big job to do.

The story of our developing a strategy and an organization for that premiere could well deserve a book of its own. After many months of hard work, the premiere was ultra successful—a full house at the Lyceum Theater for many weeks. The movie was launched. Now, perhaps I could get back to what I had originally been hired (or called, as we say in the church) to do. But no. *Martin Luther* led me in another direction that changed my life.

On the basis of the good job of executing a highly successful launching of the film, I was invited, or called, to move to New York and head the organization that had been set up to produce and distribute the movie. It was a big move. I did pray about that. I attributed the many positive signals I was getting from family and friends and professional associates as an affirmative answer to prayer. At any rate, we did move to a Long Island suburb of New York City, and I did go to work. Work? Yes, a lot of work and immediate pressure.

On the day we moved into our suburban home in Baldwin, I had to leave for six weeks in Europe to establish distribution support for 20th Century Fox, who had translated the movie into various languages and was booking it all around Europe. A year or so later, I had to do the same thing all over Latin America. For Elaine, poor soul, it was a foretaste of the next years' tolerating her peripatetic husband. Have briefcase, will travel!

Upon the success of the film, the ad hoc organization that had been set up to do the Luther film became Lutheran Film Associates, funded by the Lutheran denominations and directed by a board. Naturally the films we produced and promoted all had to have a religious content and purpose for the church to support it and for the government to grant it tax-free status.

At one point, the IRS advised Lutheran Film Associates that it was being accused of tax evasion due to the income it received through ticket sales. We certainly weren't in it for the money! I had to hire a big law firm to argue for us, on the basis that our purpose in producing the film was to advance the purposes of the church. The revenue from showings would be applied exclusively to producing other cinema projects with a religious purpose. We won! And that gave us freedom to produce other feature movies for theaters. The main one for which I was executive producer was *Question 7*, about the tension surrounding Christian work behind the Iron Curtain in East Germany. It had a respectable run in theaters in the United States and abroad. I adapted the story into my first published novel.

Another movie that made an impact in the United States was *A Time for Burning*. It told the story of an Omaha congregation troubled over how it might relate to the changing neighborhood in which it found itself. The congregation allowed us to film its meetings, discussion groups, leadership council, and energetic youth groups as they were debating the how and whether and when of racial togetherness. Filmed at the height of the 1960s social unrest related to race, *A Time for Burning* created a big stir in the papers and on television after it was shown repeatedly on public television nationwide.

In the 1970s I was finally able to produce a film on Bach. I had become an avid Bach devotee at Luther College and recognized that his glorious music was a strong Christian message proclaimed in song.

My film responsibilities morphed into broader challenges. When the separate Lutheran church bodies in our country decided they wanted to work closely together rather than competitively, they created the Lutheran Council in the USA. I was elected as the communication director for the agency. While continuing my film work via LFA, I managed a communication staff and assisted our unit leaders in public relations advice and counsel.

I felt that my status as a lay person in the church wasn't clearly understood. So many of my colleagues were clergy. Some of the time I would be called Pastor Lee, and often my mail would come addressed to the Rev. Robert E. A. Lee. Some confused me with a prominent Atlanta preacher with the same name, though without the added middle initial *A*. I once interviewed the other Robert E. Lee for WGA-TV in Atlanta. I was at the Lutheran World Federation Assembly in Helsinki, Finland, in 1963, filming from the roof of the parliament building with the cathedral and city skyline in the background. I opened the interview with "Hello from Helsinki. This is Bob Lee, and my guest today is Bob Lee—the Reverend Robert E. Lee from Peachtree Lutheran Church in Atlanta."

In my years of working within the bureaucracy of the Lutheran Church, I came to appreciate the great work the churches were doing in relief and development, especially in the third world. I sometimes chafed over management tasks. I didn't like them—budgets, planning systems, hiring and firing—but I felt I could do them well and think I did. What I really liked, however, were the opportunities to express some creativity in the arts, especially when Christian spirituality could shine through.

I had always loved the arts. I think back to those college years when KWLC at Luther College became my first open door to actual radio broadcasting. That opportunity was a neglected treasure waiting to be polished and shined. Almost no one I knew of listened regularly. So with the eager support of the faculty advisors and the college president, as well as the founder of the radio station, Oliver Eittreim (who had built the original transmitter in use when I arrived in the fall of 1938), I had more or less free rein to create programs and build an audience. It became my passion.

Some hopes and dreams are realized

In a letter of congratulation I sent in 1992 to the station manager for the sixty-fifth anniversary of KWLC, I predicted, "If I ever write my autobiography, I am sure I will credit my days of broadcast experimentation at KWLC with building a reservoir of confidence that would allow me to think that it's possible to dream dreams and have at least some of them realized."

My pastor, the Rev. Ed Barnett, preached a sermon not long ago on a Christian's vocation. He explored St. Paul's recitation in I Corinthians of the various talents and gifts given to all members of a worshipping community. As he intended, no doubt, his sermon got me thinking of my "call," the English translation of the Latin *voce*, as in "vocation."

When I was working for the Lutheran Council, I attended a staff retreat on career commitments. Each of us had to write out declarations of how we understood and defined our work challenges. I found the document I had saved and refreshed myself on my position then. I had written:

> I understand "call" as the personal mandate of service to which I dedicated myself early in my career. I interpret this on a spiritual

level as a God-supplied motivational magnetism toward the kind of activity that has as its purpose helping others; it stands over against an alternative life-engagement that is mainly focused on materialistic satisfaction.

The term "Life Mission" should embody a cause that helps people to understand and appreciate the love of God through Jesus Christ. My opportunity to pursue this "mission" happens to be in the field of communication—radio, print, news, films, video, and public relations management.

I have graduated from that religious bureaucracy, but my values and aims for sharing the positive messages of Christianity remain. For some years I had my own business that sought to assist church groups to communicate better. Some of this was in training, some in production, some in consultation. For several years I served part time as a consultant for the American Bible Society. I produced films in Latin America, the Philippines, Africa, and India for Lutheran World Relief. I prepared fund-raising videos for the Presbyterian Church. I served on national committees of Lutheran church bodies.

Now I am finding fulfillment in continuing to write. My faith, fueled by gratitude, affects this creative work. It prompts me to uncover and lay out the issues and discern how I might attack them effectively. I plan ambitiously and sketch out plots and outlines. I may plunge into research on a theme or topic, reviewing old documents and becoming almost a resident of Google and Yahoo search engines. (Where did they get those playful names?) There comes a point when I am overwhelmed by the sheer volume of material to wade through. I set it aside thinking I may get back to it but secretly knowing it's not likely I will. But sometimes inspiration breaks through, as when I explore a file that hasn't been touched for years and find a page or two of notes. I pull it out, evaluate it afresh, and conclude, "Hey, that's not a bad idea! I wonder if I can make something out of it?"

I have a limited audience for the essays and poems that I publish on my Web site, realworldcomm.com. I have had better fortune with books. Publication of the story of my mother, *Mathilda's Journey*, and the story of my late wife, *Dear Elaine*, have encouraged me to keep writing. I think I would write even if the words I compose never got published. I have always been prepared to write because it was a part of my job. Now it's something I need to do, to have an outlet for my feelings. I want to establish communication with whatever public is there.

My family has been supportive in my work all along. Now, in my retirement, they are helping me by editing, by designing and illustrating, and by making sure that their old dad has the necessary electronic equipment to help him—computers, printers, scanners, copy machines, et. al.

The creative process is a mystery and a major fascination to me. There is something spiritual about it—it doesn't fit under the scientist's microscope. There is a quality of fantasy often connected to creativity. We can let our dreams lead us—or daydreams, at least for me, since I can never remember sleep dreams, which usually escape before I am fully conscious.

I don't normally use prayer to solve creative problems, even though I believe in the power of prayer. It doesn't seem right to me to think of prayer petitions as a functional matter, as if we put the squeeze on God. Sure, I know the verses that say, "Seek and ye shall find" and "Whatsoever ye shall ask in my name, that will I do." Rather, I like to invite the working of God's divine spirit into my thinking. It is in that aspect of the Triune Godhead that inspiration comes to us. The *breath of God*. Inspiration itself means "breathing in." I imagine God breathing life into each human being, stimulating the human mind to creative thought and to the making of art.

I think about the presence of God in my life. Questions arise on the veracity of scripture's narratives and about the fascinating and sometimes fearful and almost unbelievable Old Testament characters—Adam and Eve, Noah, Jonah, Daniel, and others, confronting miracles and events that seem mythical or metaphorical rather than historical. I usually come down on the side of acceptance of such mystery. I have even less trouble with the Gospels. I am deeply impressed with the reportage of the writers who, although differing in some stories, seem to have left us a cohesive scenario of the life and even the words spoken by Jesus. I similarly appreciate what I feel is a consistency as to what happened to him before and after his death.

I find that prayer comes easily. I reject an over ritualistic formality in my prayer life. I usually just allow my soul to open up and give me the thoughts resting in my personal and altogether figurative safe-deposit box, or wherever spiritual treasures are stored. I try to enhance this religious cache from my reading scripture and inspirational literature, by regular worship with my congregation, and by the stimulating discussions about beliefs and newsworthy religious issues that are sometimes possible with thoughtful friends or with some members of my family.

Out of the depths of memory and my reservoir of theological ideas, I try to summon forth relevant words with which to voice my prayer petitions. The same source might come to my rescue when I am faced with the need to respond to a question or a provocative comment.

Ideal as this sounds, the fact has to be acknowledged that I often ignore the prayer option. I can ignore the Bible for days. I tell myself I must make a habit of spiritual exercise, just as I must admit that my habits of physical exercise are often too loosely rehearsed, to my detriment. I could call this sin. I include it among the items in my soul's waste basket to be purged through honest confession. I try to accomplish house-cleaning of this sort daily and also, in a ceremonial sense, in my liturgical worship with fellow congregants.

I believe. Help Thou my unbelief!

Don't get the idea, just because I have been rolling on about my exposure to religious communication, that I consider myself "holier than thou." Quite the contrary. The essence of my understanding of Christian faith and the Christian-influenced life is that we all are short of the mark. We err sometimes by what we do that is wrong or turns out to be wrong even if we thought it was right. Sometimes we fail or neglect to do what we should. When I have the chance, I try to make clear that the genius of the Christian life—of faith as a gift—is that it is free. It's not easy for us sinners to realize, accept, or understand that. It's in conflict with the pattern of the competitive world of commerce, of advertisements that make us want more and more and more of this and that.

Life, I have discovered, can be abundant. And for me it *is* abundant. None of it is earned. It's all free.

10 Captured by Music

I would emotionally starve without my daily infusion of music!

Music lives in my world, and I live in the world of music. This has been true for me since childhood, when I was nourished by melody. Both of my parents loved music, but neither was dependent upon it to the degree I am. My father sang, and it was legendary that he played the accordion and violin. My mother was unhappy that her sister Julia got keyboard lessons on the parlor organ; she herself never had that chance but coveted it.

My parents always had a piano, and each of us kids had a whack at it. Mom taught me to read music and where to find the notes on the keyboard, but rather than taking advantage of my chance to study seriously, I spent most of my time on the instrument improvising simple songs and sight-reading hymns and my sisters' popular songs.

My sister Juliet claims she taught me to play the piano. She was a big influence, and I loved to hear her play and have her accompany me when I sang or played the trumpet, but I never had formal lessons from her. John Bates, who was our family's official piano teacher, gave me six weeks worth of lessons. But he gave up, I think, about the time that I gave up. He and I were never simpatico. He seemed to fare better with my sisters. One or two of them thought he was a bit "fresh" (a suggestive term from those days), or maybe it was mother who sensed it.

I didn't stay with piano, but picked up the trumpet. It was my brother Bill who pushed, begged, pulled, and coerced me to join him in creating a family brass section. He taught me the elements of blowing, tonguing, and fingering the cornet (a stubby version of the trumpet), and later I did have a year or two of strong tutoring from a professional who had played in Sousa's band. When I won first place in a "national" high school trumpet competition, it was mostly because of him. I think I was a better player than I remember myself to be. If I had a polished technique once, I certainly lost it all. When I hear a great trumpeter like Marsalis or André or my good friend and college contemporary Herseth, I can't believe that I ever could cut the same music I hear from them.

And I probably didn't. But apparently I fooled a lot of folks back then who thought I did.

I never hear a strong silver blast from trumpets in a symphony orchestra—or a lovely soaring brass adagio—without a strong built-in appreciation and thrill recalling for me some of my own performance satisfaction from those days over seventy years ago.

Proud to be in Spring Grove High School Band

At first, my voice was just a secondary musical instrument. Seldom did I venture into solo singing in high school, but I heard others sing, admired and envied them, and gradually came to feel "I could do that!" When I heard a beautiful high school tenor from the nearby town of Harmony (what an appropriate name for his town!) sing "My Task," I got the music and memorized it and used it dozens of times when I was called on to perform. Thanks, pal, whoever you were. I remember hearing a baritone soloist at a concert sing "The Hills of Home" and "None But the Lonely Heart." I bought that music, too, and learned it so I could perform it respectably.

Going on to Luther College at sixteen, I was prepared to shine both as a trumpeter and as a baritone (maybe tenor, too) in that highly music-conscious and performer-focused community. Concert band was, in a way, my oyster, and I was fully confident that I could perform well. I was pretty confident about singing, too! Then I took voice lessons for the first time in my life and discovered I really didn't know how to sing. At least I wasn't doing it the right way. I learned that breath control and exploiting the vowels and other physical control tricks could make all the difference in the world. This voice training and the fact that I could read music well allowed me to become known as a legitimate musician. I had all the confidence and stage presence I needed (some would say *more* than I needed). Singing in ensembles and soloing for oratorios and operettas added to my own assurance that I had something to offer musically.

I was virtually running the radio station KWLC as an announcer. Our station was known for its good music. I would select the music. Of the programs I created where I would sing, the most lasting (it continued long after I graduated) was *Hymns We Love*, where listeners would send in their requests and Bob Lee would dedicate this or that hymn to someone named in the postcard that had been mailed to me.

My singing over KWLC radio led to some off-campus gigs (though we didn't call them that then) that were memorable opportunities for me. In September 1941, as I was entering my senior year in college, I had a call one day from Father Dostal, the Roman Catholic priest in Spillville, Iowa, near Decorah. He was a fan of mine, being a sort of "closet" listener to our Lutheran-flavored broadcasts. Spillville's claim to fame, other than the popular Bily Clock Museum, was that in the 1890s it had been the summer home of composer Antonin Dvorak, who was temporarily in this country as the head of the National Conservatory in New York. Father Dostal was in charge of the 1941 centennial celebration of Dvorak's birth, an event that would draw music lovers to Spillville. He invited me to sing with the orchestra he was importing from Minnesota's Twin Cities. To me that sounded wonderfully challenging. He had a book of Dvorak's biblical songs, and he asked if I would be willing to sing one of his favorites in it. Sure! But it had only piano accompaniment. While I had never made an orchestral arrangement, I knew enough about them to sense that I could do it. And so I did. I still have the score and some of the instrumental parts that I copied out. It was "Turn to Me" from Psalm 17. I had never seen nor heard the music before, but Clara Hoyt, my voice teacher, coached me, and I felt confident. At the radio station I also found the orchestral music for Dvorak's "Songs My Mother Taught Me." Both songs went well, and I was flattered by all the attention the performance garnered, including a front page picture and story in the *Decorah Journal* and a review in the *Des Moines Register* that included this reference to me: "A lad named Robert E. Lee poured out "Songs My Mother Taught Me" in a golden baritone."

Of course I didn't travel my musical journey alone. I met and married a brilliant, naturally gifted musician. Elaine Naeseth could have been the campus musical queen, if they had had such an honor then. A storybook beginning to a life of love and music.

While in college I had some aspirations toward a professional career in music. But I finally realized that I wasn't *that* good. And other interests were waiting in the wings, or already on stage. Broadcasting. Films. Communication. Writing. No immediate choice was needed or possible because World War II likewise was waiting in the wings. Waiting, as it turned out, *with* wings for me.

In the Navy, too, I had opportunities to sing. I entered a talent contest that was broadcast on a local Minneapolis radio station. My accompanist from WCCO was to help me choose some music, as I didn't have any sheet music among my few personal effects. He brought with him to our rehearsal a new pop tune, "As Time Goes By," that had just been featured in the Humphrey Bogart-Ingrid Bergman movie, *Casablanca*. I won the contest and a fifty dollar war bond—a lot of cash in those days—but I never saw the money.

Later, at the Naval Air Station in Corpus Christi, Texas, several of us cadets put together a musical revue with parodies, skits, and songs. We called our entertainment evening "Life at Easy Acres," a not-too-subtle dig at our specialized training base, which had a reputation for being brutally demanding. One of us—I wish I remembered his name—was an outstanding pianist, and he and I got an enthusiastic response to "Begin the Beguine" and some other encore tunes.

Even out in the Pacific aboard ship, I sang at chapel services at the request of the chaplain. That setting for worship was unique: we were gathered together in the midst of a dangerous war zone. We all were aware that some of us might not be at the next chapel service. Therefore, the hymns, the songs, and the prayers had special meaning.

After the war, I used my music training and background several important times in my career of film producing. When shooting *Question 7* in Germany in the spring and summer of 1960, we had in the script some scenes with singing. One was an episode including the Freie Deutsche Jugend (Free German Youth), a Communist youth league in what was then the red nation of East Germany. As they marched with drums and flags flying, we needed the parading young men to sing both in their native German and in our English (for American and British audiences). It was my task to find the right song, translate the German into lyrical English, and—since the young men didn't speak English—teach it to them by means of phonetic equivalent sounds. Also, when the congregation was worshipping and singing a hymn, we filmed and recorded two versions; I supervised the German and taught them (again, phonetically) to sing the same hymn in English. Of course there are some syllables that Germans have difficulty in pronouncing in English—I can still hear the congregation singing "If zhou but suffer God to guide zhee."

Later, when I proposed doing a film on Johann Sebastian Bach and our board agreed to finance the fourth scenario we worked up, then it was my job to supervise the development, scripting, and realization of the film. I loved it. Bach was my favorite music, and I was happy to deal with the wonderful community of musicians. It was that enviable roster of artists who helped make *Joy of Bach* such a hit on TV and video.

I feel so fortunate to have mingled on numerous occasions with musicians of exceptional talent, some of them famous. In addition to the respect, admiration, and friendship I feel for them, they mirror the kind of the musical purity I most admire.

My friend Adolf "Bud" Herseth of the Chicago Symphony, although now retired, still ranks among the top musicians in the country. Elaine and I were pleased to visit him backstage in the Green Room at Carnegie Hall and Avery Fisher Hall in Manhattan, and earlier at the Northrup Auditorium at the University of Minnesota. His performance at Ravinia accompanied me every morning for years as I exercised to the recording of the well-known Hummel trumpet concerto.

In the realm of spiritual music, I think of my longtime friends, hymn writer Carl Schalk and his librettist Jaroslav Vajda. Carl and I were on the board of the Lutheran Music Program together. I see their faces as I sing some of their hymns in the Lutheran hymnals that we have at home and at church.

Looking back over my world of music, I realize how very significant our *Hausmusik* was. Elaine was at the piano, Peg with her flute and string bass, Barbara with her cello, and Sigrid with recorder, flute, vielle and viola da gamba. (She is the one professional musician emerging from our family.) In addition, we had Richard with his French horn and Sylvia with her silken soprano and contralto. Paul had a go at it, too, with some piano lessons, but never felt compelled to follow it up. Nor would he sing. But we knew he could, as sometimes we would hear him humming a tune or even voicing the words if he thought no one was overhearing. He remains a music lover, but is more wide-ranging in his musical taste than his father and is especially skilled at selecting just the right music for slide shows, videos, or family gatherings.

Now, as a widower finally retired, I still feast on music. I find a private haven at the piano. I'm not a pianist in the formal sense of the term. But I love to play and can read simple music. I have a special relationship with Johann Sebastian Bach. Early on I discovered, almost by accident, that I could read some of Bach's seemingly simple pieces in the Anna Magdalena Songbook. That led to other Bach works that were playable, provided no controlling metronome was clicking out a tempo faster than I could follow. That experience taught me that my friend Bach has a special present for those of us who are able to discover that translating the notes from the page to the keys is more than half of the pleasure. That is, the process of playing Bach becomes more important than the resulting sound that might reach other ears than our own.

I had the joy of being in Sebastian's hometown, Leipzig, to help the world celebrate Bach's 300th birthday in 1985. Talk about a festival! There were concerts all over the place, including at the St. Thomas Church. I'll never forget the closing concert of that celebration. Kurt Masur conducted the *St. Matthew Passion* in the Gewandhaus. It is not overstating it to say the music was heavenly. When it concluded, following that lamenting lullaby that rises spiritually as a glorious memorial to the Crucified One, there was absolute silence. Maestro Masur did not turn to the audience. What was wrong? Why was he so reluctant? Then finally, when the audience began its thunderous and unrelenting applause anyway, he turned and, without acknowledging the laudation for himself, took the manuscript and held it aloft. We all celebrated the genius, the great Bach, and our friend, Sebastian.

I love to sing, and my home church choir has welcomed me. I have loved the opportunity to sight-read and participate in our musical offering, but I have now retired from choir singing. When I was asked to record my voice the other day, I was aghast at how strident it sounded, especially in comparison to my earlier "golden baritone." I often wonder whether I could have maintained the voice quality if I had done some singing practice each day. The same is true for my diminishing urge to sit down at the piano. I diddle at the keyboard now and then, but I try not to be overheard. My fingers just don't do what they once did. The situation is improving, however, because I acquired a new piano, and that has made my fingers limber up more.

"The song is ended, but the melody lingers on."

Musik's Mystery

Come and play
music with me
Not a childish game
Still we play
or try to
More than sound we hear
We listen
Inspired excited
pleasured pleased
Or not
Spiritual somehow
mysterious
Beyond description
Beyond definition
Remote clicks
bring instant mystery
Hi-Fi's Lo-Fi's
Melody rivulets
Heart-beating rhythms
infuse into veins
Invade memory cells
Inhabit gene strings
Shall we dance?

Bach Beethoven Brahms
Mozart Mahler Mendelssohn
Sing to us
Invade our souls
Despite off-clicking
radio CD tape
computer
Despite leaving
Carnegie Alice Avery
Memory replay touched
"Hearing" while we walk
Shower
Lie on pillows
Perchance to dream?
Name that tune—
which cantata?
Symphony suite sonata?
Soprano song singer star?
O Mother Mystery
Come play with me
Sister son soul mate
Come pray with me

God will explain music

Will music explain God?

11 ON THE ROAD WITH MARTIN LUTHER

The great reformer Martin Luther had a hold on me that lasted over fifty years. Yes, I'm a Lutheran—I belong to that Protestant denomination that takes its name from the sixteenth century monk who took on the Pope and split the church. But I'm not talking about Luther's theological dominance in my life; I mean *Martin Luther,* the movie.

The Lutheran Church was prominent among the religious communities, so it was natural that its members began suggesting, "Why don't we tell the life of Martin Luther on film?" This was quickly seized upon as a good idea. Paul Empie of the National Lutheran Council invited screenwriter Allen Sloane to develop a script. When representatives from about half a dozen separate Lutheran groups in the United States and Canada began talking about it with big-time movie producers, they found more interest than they expected. Louis deRochemont reacted with enthusiasm. He was well known both for his feature theatrical movies (*Fighting Lady* and *Lost Boundaries*) and documentaries (*March of Time*). He convinced Empie and the Lutheran film board that the Luther story was ripe for theatrical cinema treatment. It would, however, cost more than they had thought. Even so, the movie was totally financed by our churches, and with a modest budget deRochemont accomplished the production and delivered a hit film later recognized as a classic.

I was selected back in 1953 as the point person to make sure that the new cinema product was seen by the most people possible in theaters and on television around the world. An important additional format was 16 mm (about half the size of theatrical 35 mm film). At the time churches and schools used this smaller size, but the process was still quite cumbersome: the projectionist had to haul out and unpack the heavy projector and its big reels. From these reels a long ribbon loaded with an array of tiny, tiny replicated photographic images unrolled through a wee aperture. The film ribbon was edged by a narrow optical sound track, so that, with lamp and lens, a talking movie image was projected onto a portable screen. Some years later in order that the film could continue to reach its audience, it was transferred to video tape cassettes to be shown on TV monitors. More recently the Luther film was reproduced on DVD.

In movie theaters *Martin Luther* not only was seen by record audiences, it produced a profit at the box office. However, it raised hackles with a lot of people. The very controversy, ironically, created new audiences and helped to make the movie a major success. It didn't happen automatically. Many people worked hard to promote it.

Here's how I got involved: I was on the board of Lutheran Church Productions, the unit set up by the Lutheran bodies in the United States that came together to create the film. Our board commissioned deRochemont Associates, with Lothar Wolff in charge as the producer. He engaged a Hollywood director and actors from the United Kingdom, France, and Germany. As a board member, I critiqued the script and several revised drafts, as well as the rough cut. Back in Minneapolis, I was busy with other tasks and was confident that the main players in New York would do their best to get it screened for the public.

The head of the deRochemont organization, F. Borden Mace, and the Lutheran church's pioneer film executive, Henry Endress, brought the finished movie to our town. They had figured that Minnesota, with all its Lutherans, would be the ideal place to launch the movie. Some of us who were in the private screening they had set up discussed that possibility. Frankly, I discouraged it. I ticked off a number of points where I thought their plan would run into problems and might not work. Then, surprise! They pointed at me and said, "We want you to handle it." After my negative comments I had thought I was not their likely candidate. But they responded, "You're the only one who raised the right questions and realized all that needed to be done."

My plate was already full. But they went to my boss and convinced him. He said he wanted me to do it. I was drafted. Of course it changed my life—particularly after the world premiere, which I organized and directed, proved to be a phenomenal success. We had lots of publicity, long lines in front of the theater for a month, and busloads of viewers coming in from our state and from Wisconsin and South Dakota as well. Reviews were glowing. The trade press, *Variety* and the others, declared that *Martin Luther* was a hot box office booking. Show business talking about box office is the key. If a movie won't make money, forget it.

In New York, the Lutheran staff working with the film makers were overwhelmed with the demand for the movie throughout the country. They were planning showings abroad as well. When I went to the next meeting, Oswald Hoffmann, one of the key board members, took me aside and said, "We want you to come to New York and manage the world distribution of this movie for us." It turned out to be an offer I couldn't refuse.

So, I closed up shop in Minneapolis. I left behind my *Children's Chapel* programs, my supervision of the new PR department, and the management of ELC

Films, the small film company I was running. Elaine and I, now with four kids, had to be realistic in recognizing that this was a major move—half way across the nation—that would command my attention, time, energy, and talents. It was urgent that I begin. We went with the expectation that it might continue for a year or two, and then we could come back and resume life as Midwesterners.

Wrong. I was hooked by *Luther* in a custodial relationship that would indeed continue for a half century.

I should explain that the religious climate back in the 1950s was tense. There was genuine antagonism between Protestants (including us Lutherans) and Roman Catholics. The Roman church went on the attack in many places. Their press denounced the movie as false and malicious and warned their flocks not to see it. In Protestant circles, the opposite was true. The word was out that our film, based on the historical record and not fictionalized, exposed the rather gross and brutal practices of virtually the only Western Christian church of that medieval time. It focused on the very issues that the monk Luther objected to. He dared to challenge the Pope, and his protests took off with the help of tracts made possible by Gutenberg's invention of the printing press.

Thus one of my immediate concerns was to issue statements defending the authenticity of the movie. We had the help of some of the best theologians, historians, and biographers of Luther—Roland Bainton from Yale, for example—who made a compelling defense of the truth of the historical material upon which the script was based. To be sure, drama thrives on conflict, and the movie brought out the severe tension within the religious life in the sixteenth century. It was a period of fear and ecclesiastical abuse, with damnation bans issued against the reformers. Even the emperor (Charles V of the Holy Roman Empire, which dominated most of Europe in that era) got involved. Luther was brought before his throne (called the Diet at Worms) for trial and punishment. It was the brave and adamant "Here I stand" position of Brother Martin that the world remembers. Before he could be jailed, however, he was secretly rescued by a friendly prince and protected in Wartburg castle until it was safe for him to re-enter society. But it wasn't really safe, because there was a warrant out for his arrest, dead or alive!

The story is compelling. Viewers discovered so much they could identify with and relate to. *Martin Luther*'s box office progress as a film was aided not only by praise from the critics but also by its nomination for Academy Awards in the photography and scenic design categories.

My family might have wanted an Oscar nomination for the *Martin Luther* film's costuming. Several years after the filming was completed, the special monks' robes and even the pope's vestments were sent to our office in New York. What to do with them? I decided to take them home and store them in our basement. After they had been lying there unpacked for a year or two, we decided that we might as well use them for Halloween costumes! So our kids would parade through the neighborhood with their trick-or-treat bags, dressed as Augustinian monks or Catholic prelates.

About four years later, it was time to premiere the movie for television. In those days there was a longer gap in time between theater release and TV screenings of theatrical movies. I was able to get a contract for showing with one of the big TV outlets in Chicago, WGN, operated by the powerful *Chicago Tribune*. We had lots of cooperation from the Protestant community there, and a strong committee was formed to publicize and promote the TV premiere. Good TV ratings would help us spread it further, of course.

Our plans were frustrated at the last minute, and a major controversy erupted. The management of WGN had presumably been warned that the Roman Catholic diocese of Chicago would vehemently oppose the showing. I was on the next plane to Chicago. It was just a few days until the broadcast. We held furious sessions about this, and pressure was exerted on WGN and the *Tribune*. But to no avail. The telecast was canceled. An avalanche of negative publicity rained on the station and the newspaper. What to do? I had a valid contract, but what good would a lawsuit accomplish? Finally we were able to get a sponsor and prime time on a competing Chicago TV outlet. And we did an end run around WGN and copped a larger audience than we might have expected without that publicity-gaining controversy.

About this time our film unit was getting urgent requests from rental libraries that served church and educational organizations with teaching films, most in 16 mm. They couldn't often use full-length feature movies, but *Martin Luther* was different. A new concept for reaching those institutional audiences was created. It wasn't my idea to begin with. Our treasurer and Borden Mace, the head of deRochemont, proposed to me that we make a massive effort to sell—not rent—the complete film (in 16 mm format) to individual congregations at a low rate. While normally such movies over one hour in length (Luther had a running time of 105 minutes) would cost $500 or more, we would sell the film outright to churches at $150, and they could show it over and over as many times and for as many years as the print would last. We had the help of an ad agency to give us some effective mailing pieces. We bought mailing lists to include thousands of local congregations. We were aiming the release for Reformation Day at the end of October, when many congregations observe the birthday of Protestantism.

It worked. Not only did it work, it overwhelmed my office with orders. I had to get extra staff to help get the orders out. They were shipped from a laboratory in Hollywood, but orders and payment came to us in New York. Overtime and more. It was one of the most anxiety-laden experiences during my time as custodian and manager of *Martin Luther*.

While the Luther film continued to be popular, my office went on to prepare and produce other movies, both for internal showings within churches and for public showings, mostly on television and later on video cassettes and, even more recently, on DVD formats. I edited and published a book using the excellent black and white still pictures from *Martin Luther*—not copied from the movie negatives, but rather taken by a skilled camera artist during the production. From the scripts I was able to select text to summarize the content that the many photographs described.

After fifty years the Luther Film was still being shown

We recycled Luther several times. We released for churches a teaching version that had introductions and explanations by Yale historian Bainton. We also created a condensed version of the movie by depicting abridged material from the long film. That half-hour summary was sufficient for those interested in learning about the details of the Protestant Reformation. And later I composed a series of four fifteen-minute tapes, *Luther Legacy*, narrated by Bill Whitney, a prominent CBS newscaster. The life of the original film also included its being translated into other languages. I toured Latin America to introduce Luther there. We dubbed the sound track into Spanish in Mexico City. Yes, bringing *Martin Luther* down below the border was like invading the territory of the enemy. But the only place where we had trouble was in Brazil, where the movie was banned by the government censor. As usual the ban created interest for many to want to see what all the fuss was about.

Other bans were imposed (and mostly circumvented by cooperating churches) in the Philippines and in Montreal, Quebec. There also the head of the provincial government personally signed the ban. Eleven churches responded by opening their doors to any of the public wanting to see *Luther*. The Canadian edition of *Time* ran a cover picture of crowds pouring into a Presbyterian church in Montreal.

Our movie was also banned in an unlikely place: India. There the problem had nothing to do with the Roman Catholic objection. Rather the censor wanted to cut out the scenes of angry iconoclasts smashing statues and breaking church windows. The Indian government had a campaign against violence, and presumably felt that this action would encourage internecine tension there (e.g. Hindu-Muslim rioting). Our distributor in India solved the issue by allowing the censors to excise those offending scenes. Again some newspaper stories about it became good publicity.

I certainly got an education about Reformation history and the life of Martin Luther in particular. I suppose I had to watch the film hundreds of times. I had memorized much of the dialogue and knew the background music and just where it was cued to come in. In addition, I had to write study material to go with the film and articles for many church publications and even radio and television interviews on occasion.

During all of this memorializing of the Reformer—millions would learn of his historic influence on history and religion from seeing the movie—it was inescapable that Luther's angry and dismissive comments on Jews would also meet the light of day. Controversy came. Not only did I expect the subsequent accusations of anti-Semitism, but I found they were not altogether inaccurate. He was guilty, at least on twentieth century terms. His defenders pointed to the fact that his condemnation was theological—Luther's reaction to the Jewish rejection of Jesus as the Messiah. But more acknowledgment of his culpability by us Lutherans was called for.

In response to a letter in the *New York Times*, I wrote a response that was subsequently printed:

> A Time to Study the Whole of Martin Luther
>
> To the Editor:
>
> It is true, as Prof. Brickman complains (letter of Nov. 11), that Martin Luther had some intemperate and inflammatory words to say about Jews. But he was equally abusive to others. He reserved some of his worst epithets for the papacy.
>
> As the 500th anniversary of Luther's birth is observed in 1983, much will be said and written about this giant of history, who shook the world with his theological theses. His supporters and critics can and will discuss and argue why, in the context of the turbulent 16th century, so brilliant a theologian, preacher, linguist, and teacher should rail so excessively against his perceived religious enemies. But it is hoped that during the jubilee year Luther's historically pivotal doctrines and their consequences will be confronted as well.
>
> Robert E. A. Lee
Director of Communication
Lutheran Council in the U.S.A.
New York, Dec. 3, 1982

Indeed, later on, the largest U. S. Lutheran body did seriously study the issue and, as a result, issued a public declaration in the 1990s formally rejecting Luther's position on the Jews. The then-presiding bishop of the Evangelical Lutheran Church in America made a pilgrimage to Israel to formally present the document to the religious and political establishments.

The week-long celebration of the 500th birthday of Luther kept me extremely busy before, during, and after. Luther was born in Eisleben, Germany, in 1485 on November 10, and the celebration was to take place during the week of November 10, 1985. Although we could not get another movie ready by then, I proposed that, instead, we stage a theatrical event. My LFA board and the Jubilee committee liked that idea. So I enlisted my team veterans, who had collaborated in producing *The Joy of Bach*, for a flurry of creativity. Lothar Wolfe, Allan Sloane, and Paul Lammers were willing to join me to come up with a pageant-like show we chose to call *A Parade of Witnesses*. It was Sloane's idea that we could have a series of tableaux from Luther's life. Witnesses from that era and from later years would comment favorably and unfavorably on various dramatic vignettes.

We were given a most unusual location for our Washington D.C. production: The Roman Catholic Shrine of the Immaculate Conception! It was a huge space with plenty of room for the staged presentation, plus a powerful pipe organ. The irony of this palace of Roman ecclesiastical authority being the host for this presentation was not lost. It was to honor the man who fought the Pope in the sixteenth century and was excommunicated and condemned. Ecumenism had come a long way!

Lammers, with his CBS contacts, helped us arrange for a satellite feed, in those days still relatively innovative. Even though we had no traditional network to host us on cable channels, we decided to create our own network. I hired Tommy Thompson, who had been a *Lutheran Hour* executive, to develop agreements with local outlets throughout the nation to pick up and rebroadcast the hour and a half program from Washington, D.C. via satellite. It worked!

I approached David Soul of *Starsky and Hutch* TV fame to be our Luther. In earlier conversations with him I had discovered he really wanted to interpret that role. He accepted right away and offered his talents gratis. He in turn helped us cast Mim Solberg as Luther's wife, Katy. We enlisted Shakespearean repertory actors from Washington, who were excellent in recreating the historical characters in our witness parade.

The president of Luther College was our narrator. Dr. H. George Anderson was lively and convincing as he set the stage and played well both to the TV cameras and to the audience. (Anderson later became the presiding bishop of the national Lutheran denominational group known as the Evangelical Lutheran Church in America.) In the shrine's pews were many international dignitaries of both Lutheran and other Protestant groups.

The days and hours of preparation did pay off. The mounting of the show, with only a partial dress rehearsal possible, was a pressure cooker. As a director of live and recorded television drama, Paul Lammers was more than equal to the task. When the dress rehearsal told him that we were almost a half-hour over time, he had our team meet to make big block cuts—whole scenes were eliminated, much to the sorrow of those ready to play.

During that memorable week I produced a video short on *Luther Experts on Luther*, since most of the world's most prominent Lutheran scholars were there to participate. In contrast, I also created a light comic musical as entertainment before the formal dinner for the Jubilee week.

In the first few years of the twenty-first century, a new movie about the Reformer was made. It carried the similar, but simplified, title of *Luther*. I was also drawn into that project. I had no official role (I really had, finally, retired), but I did serve as a consultant to the German producers. However, I declined an offer to participate in the filming abroad as an advisor. It came at a time when Elaine was very ill and I could not leave her. I felt the film should have a different story line, but after trying various alternatives to our 1952 production, the new movie ended up with a story parallel to the one we had delivered fifty years before. There was a good reason for that. It turned out that the most dramatic part of Martin Luther's life had really climaxed sixteen years before he died. The basic story of the revolt was technically and dramatically over by the time the princes of Germany gave solid support to the followers of Luther. The height of the action was the courageous rebellion of the princes against the Holy Roman Empire. It came to be known as the Augsburg Confession of 1530.

While I didn't write the new Luther movie that starred Joseph Fiennes in the lead role, nor have any lingering responsibility for it as before, I did make one contribution that I feel was essential to making it a good film and a success. After considerable searching and consulting, I found for the producers the screenwriter I believed could do the best job. Camille Thomasson was more than equal to the task and, in my view, accomplished it beautifully.

Brother Martin—oops, Dr. Luther—who presided over the historic Reformation, was an enigmatic and complex character: brilliant, even a genius of sorts, charismatic, bold, and irascible. He was kind and loving but also volatile and stubborn, bitter and vindictive. He railed against those he saw as enemies of the cross: the Pope, the Turks (read Muslims), and the Jews. He was a prolific writer, turning out theses, sermons, catechisms, Bible studies, and even songs such as "A Mighty Fortress is Our God" and "From Heaven Above to Earth I Come." The first Luther film actor, Niall MacGinnis, and the most recent, Joseph Fiennes, could not be more different in appearance and personality as revealed on the screen. Yet each of them in his own way was a skillful actor who could make me believe that he *was* Luther. They were consummate professional British thespians. I learned from each. I shall never forget the heritage that each movie communicated—probably very few viewers have seen both, as I have. I now know better why I am a Lutheran. I hope I can live by the lines of my film that have reverberated in my memory through this half century: "No man can command my conscience!"

And I remember the slogan we placed on our billboards and newspaper ads so many years ago: THE MAN WHO CHANGED THE WORLD … FOREVER!

12 Moviemaking Magic

I grew up in the era when both radio broadcasting and movies sneaked into our cultural and economic scene and soon became an entertainment passion for millions. As a child I dreamed of someday being on the air myself and maybe acting in, or at least creating movie stories. I wanted to be big time! Who doesn't at that tender age? But the motivation and the fascination stuck. In my own humble way, I have been able to use these media to tell stories and communicate something worthwhile to others.

In the first decade of my life, 1921-1931, AM radio was coming of age and catching on quickly to embrace almost everybody. When our family gathered around our Atwater Kent or Philco radio, we laughed at and loved Amos and Andy, George Burns and Gracie Allen, Eddie Cantor, Kate Smith, Bing Crosby, and even Walter Damrosch with his symphony concerts.

While I was a radio announcer at the commercial station WMIN, our station, as well as hundreds of others, made a transition by adding FM to the AM spectrum. Both had advantages: AM bounced off the skies, so that could we sit in our living rooms and tune in an AM signal from "clear channel" stations in Nashville or Del Rio, Texas. In contrast, FM, which grew out of World War II technology, had a greater fidelity to sound reproduction and the absence of static. But FM was limited by line of sight transmission. That meant that the competition was strictly local. A plethora of FM stations grew up all over the country, so that almost every community could be served. Soon we all realized that radio broadcasting and movies were somehow merging into still another art form—television. And yes, I wanted to be along for that ride also.

My broadcasting experience had been the prelude to my additional fascination with communicating via film. I'm glad I had been around to experience the excitement when movies first added sound. The first theater projectors had big phonograph platters synchronized (not always successfully in those early days) to play in lock-step with the moving picture so that when persons on the screen were seen talking, we accepted it as natural. Then came color. Technicolor movies could be charming and enchanting—except when done badly, and then they could be sickening. Actors might appear to be in the "pink"—literally, if not figuratively. Even though some early processes had colorized movies in the previous decades, the first all color and sound film didn't come to theaters until 1928. Because the process was difficult and expensive, few films could risk it. Disney with his cartoons led the way.

While I had a few cheap home movie cameras, both 8 mm and 16 mm, I quickly learned that my forte was not operating the camera. It was not until after World War II (when everything changed!) that my first crack at helping to produce movies came in Minneapolis. I was already in radio work there, news and public relations for the national Lutheran Church. When Paul Rusten involved me in his ELC films projects, I found it a to be a wonderful experimental laboratory. I had directed radio drama but never a film story. But that didn't stop me—the principles are much the same.

One of my acquaintances from Luther College had become a successful actress in New York. Georgeann Johnson had a good role in a weekly TV show, *Mr. Peepers*, a 50s network comedy, and she also played on Broadway, once opposite Henry Fonda. We had been commissioned to do a half-hour film for a women's missionary group, and I thought it would be wonderful if we could get her to "star" in our modest production. While we couldn't really pay her, maybe she was successful enough so she might donate her talents. We offered to fly her out to Minneapolis from New York. To our surprise and delight, Georgeann said yes. I know she agreed purely out of friendship for me. My older daughters will never forget that when I picked her up at the airport, I brought her to our house so she could join us for breakfast! We got the film made, and Georgeann was perfect and a joy to work with. Whatever happened to that special little production? What was its title? Maybe today it lies in a dusty archive somewhere.

When I was co-opted to launch the world premiere for *Martin Luther* in Minneapolis, there I was with a full length, feature movie, whose destiny was more or less in my hands. I didn't need to understand all about film making to do that job, which was largely promotional. I used the techniques of public relations and journalism (and a lot of common sense) to get teams of helpers to work together. It was a task similar to putting together a show on the stage or on the air. In my next national assignment for the church, running our Lutheran film production company, the tasks were largely related to promotion and public relations as well—getting the movie shown all over the world. The church looked to me for leadership in what film project might be next.

I had a pretty good ride in the 1960s, 70s and 80s, with major film undertakings as well as smaller in-house flicks. I was also asked to produce some films as freelance projects. When Luther College asked me to help them produce some recruiting films, I was glad to comply. For one of them I used daughter Sigrid's musical talent to record a theme song that she and I worked out, with music she sang to her own guitar accompaniment. I found this fulfilling, not only because I was working for my *alma mater*, but because Sigrid did a beautiful job and I was proud of her. Those personal projects, as well as the short films I produced for the church, provided me with good experience for the freelance work I was called upon to do after my formal retirement.

I didn't really retire. Rather I formed my own consulting and production company doing business as REALWorld Communications. I didn't have to search for projects. They came to me. I did a lot of traveling, producing videos for organizations I knew well from my earlier days.

For Lutheran World Relief, I made several trips to the Philippines and prepared the video *Filipino Dream*, describing the various development projects to help the indigenous tribes there. Living with the mountain folks for a week or more was a great experience. I learned how eager those Filipinos were to better their lives, to learn techniques that not only produce more agricultural food but also help rather than harm the environment. "Slash and burn" had for years been the acceptable style for them, but it eroded the mountainsides and caused catastrophic mud slides when the monsoon rains came.

There was one dramatic scene I couldn't use. We filmed the resident regent of the mountain tribe on the island of Mindanao at a thanksgiving ritual for a good harvest. While drums were beating out a hypnotic rhythm, the "king" took a live chicken to sacrifice. While the camera zoomed in to memorialize forever the moment of decapitation of the screeching fowl—the *coup de grâce*—all bloody hell broke loose: blood everywhere, with tribal explosions of ecstasy, shouting, and dancing. Not exactly appropriate for viewing before (or after) church suppers!

LWR also wanted somehow to advise the good people of congregations as to how their offerings were providing help and hope in Africa, Asia, and Latin America. So we developed a concept I called *Windows of Hope*. These were five-minute vignettes reflecting some aspect of overseas help provided by Lutherans in America. We ran the gamut of projects in South India, in the Sahel area of West Africa, in rural markets and disease-ridden slums in Kenya. High in the Andes of Peru we showed how sanitation could help avoid diseases like cholera, and in Honduras how ancient herb gardens could be adapted so as to be fully compatible with modern medical knowledge.

I was told that the most popular film LWR ever distributed was my video entitled *Flying Quilts*. We showed how women in local churches had quilting bees on a regular basis and would make hundreds of colorful quilts which were shipped off somewhere in the world where needy people could be comforted and warmed by them. I decided not just to show the quilting, packing, and shipping processes, but how these quilts were actually used somewhere in the world. I found a Roman Catholic hospital in Tanzania where LWR quilts covered every bed in the hospital—about the only place for miles around where ill people could be treated. The doctor there and the nurses were effusive in their thanks to their Lutheran friends in the United States who provided these quilts which they called "life-saving." I admit it made a fine visual story. My family helped with this video also: my son-in-law Chris composed the music to the film's theme song, which my daughter Sylvia sang over the opening and closing credits. I loved it.

Sometimes, rather than seeking research for a story we had planned, we had a compelling idea come to us. When we were first researching our planned Bach movie, we visited Bach sites in the East half of Germany. When we went over to the East (officially named the German Democratic Republic), we discovered another subject that had more timely cinematic relevance for our Lutheran church. The Christian church behind the Iron Curtain, consisting mostly of our Lutheran brothers and sisters, was still fighting a kind of war that they called the *Kirkenkampf*, or religious battle—not with the Nazis this time but with the Communists. We talked to pastors and church members who were stifled in their freedom to worship, whose youth were being seduced into party membership, where even parents of infants were pressured into skipping baptism ceremonies in favor of state-sponsored rituals of "name-giving ceremonies." Our Luther film scriptwriter, Allan Sloane (himself once accused in the United States of being a "fellow traveler"), felt strongly that we should make a movie about the crisis our Lutherans over there were living through. He had talked in secret with pastors who had been threatened and even jailed. He wanted to write that script. Bach could wait, he argued. Our board agreed and asked him to go to work.

Sloane came up with a script based on true stories that he had researched. These were to result in our next major production, the theatrical film *Question 7*. It was my job to make it happen. The board voted the funds—never enough, of course—and we went to work. Because we had had such good fortune working with producer Lothar Wolff of DeRochemont Associates on *Martin Luther*, we engaged him again. He had been born in Berlin and had left as a refugee from Hitler. Once we had the right screenplay draft—revised many times—Lothar was able to negotiate with German technicians for the filming.

One charming town between Hamburg and Lübeck was Mölln, famous for being the site of the legendary Till Eulenspiegel, the elfin personality whose merry pranks were made famous by composer Richard Strauss. Town officials agreed to let us re-decorate their town to represent Osterstadt, a fictional East German community, for the purpose of filming. We knew that the East German government would never allow our film to be made in the East, as it was critical of the Communist regime. They must have been worried about our movie. We were later alarmed to discover that they had a spy among us who reported on our activities. We were even able to hear East German radio newscasts telling wild stories about what was going on where we were—just across the border in the West.

It was a rare experience for me to see the British/German/French actors performing our drama, as directed by Hollywood's Stuart Rosenberg. *Question 7* was the story of Peter, the son of a Lutheran pastor, who was caught between the pressures of his Christian family and his Communist teachers. He wanted to please both and found that he could not. He was a gifted pianist who, against his parents' better judgment, was allowed to enter a musical contest in Berlin. And it was there that he was persuaded by his conscience to defect through the Brandenburg Gate to freedom in the West.

Once the film was released and we realized that the press reviews and the public reaction were good, I had to travel like crazy around the U.S.A. making arrangements for volunteer supporters to help us create larger audiences. We imported two of our actors from Germany—Almut Eggert and Erik Schumann—to add some glamour to our promotion and publicity. They were interviewed and photographed to help build curiosity for *Question 7*. It worked, even though we couldn't match the amazing success of our *Luther* venture.

My next big task was quite different. While we were evaluating dozens of subjects and story lines for another big theatrical film project, the American Missions units of our Lutheran churches pleaded with us to try to produce a film that would speak to a burning issue. They were alarmed by this new domestic crisis—growing racial tension. This was in the midst of the turbulent 1960s, a time of civil rights protests and angry street scenes with fire hoses and police dogs and marches and even killings. They wanted a film showing a Christian perspective on this problem. At least, they said, give us a tool that will help our churches, our people, to rise positively to the challenge.

No simple nor easy task, that. Who had all the wisdom to say just what was needed and what would work? I quickly convened a series of one-day conferences in a half dozen American cities, North, South, East, and West, inviting pastors and lay persons of both races to sit down together and talk about how they could reflect the situation where they were. Many of these folks had not known one another before. The sessions—all recorded and transcribed verbatim—were not confrontational, but participants were urged to be candid and honest and forthright in sharing what they were experiencing on various sides of these questions. The comments were highly revealing. I worked long and hard, with a team of helpers, to discover from this material what might help synthesize the essence of these meetings. We learned that it wasn't all a North-South polarity: sometimes there was more segregation north of the Mason-Dixon line than south.

We proposed that we be permitted to film a congregation within a community where the racial balance was changing. We located one in Omaha, Nebraska. The pastor of Augustana Lutheran Church, founded by Swedish Lutheran immigrants, was Bill Youngdahl. He had worked in social ministry for the national church and was savvy about what was going on in Omaha: plenty of racial bias below the calm surface. And he knew that, in recently coming to that church, he had the challenge of trying to make a difference. Youngdahl helped us to convince his congregation that we could look over their shoulders with our cameras as they tried to deal with the sensitive and difficult traditional and emotional undercurrents.

We were fortunate to interest Bill Jersey, a brilliant documentary film maker who was pioneering a then-new approach called *cinema vérité*. He and his associate Barbara Connell were sharp, creative, highly competent, and professional—and also kind and sensitive human beings. They caught amazing moments that by themselves seem almost pedestrian, but in the context of the situation, the moments became infused with powerful emotion.

The resulting documentary, *A Time for Burning*, found its way to public broadcasting's NET, the predecessor in the 1960s of PBS. It woke up America. The press pounced on this story; its coverage and its large TV audience were amazing to us and to the television industry. Our movie was even nominated for an Oscar at the Academy Awards. After its runs on television, it had a wide distribution as a videocassette and later as a DVD. For decades, *A Time for Burning* has remained as an exemplary documentary, considered by many as a classic. It has been referred to in books and has been reintroduced in film festivals. In 2005 it was recognized by the Library of Congress as worthy of inclusion in the National Film Register.

After the flow of success following *A Time for Burning*, a Bach film possibility rose again to the surface in my thinking. For over a dozen years through the 1950s and 1960s, it had been simmering in my unconsciousness. It seemed that each year brought Bach's music further forward in the public's purview. I wanted to try again. By this time I had finished a manuscript, *Bach in Season*, as well as several articles about Bach.

The breakthrough came during a session in Bermuda with a wise group of consultants that included writers, musicians, critics, and film and television specialists. Eureka! This group unanimously concurred that the music of Bach, rather than the composer's biography, should be—must be—the "star" of our film. While not ignoring the man in his time and place, the drama of what has happened to Bach's music should be the story, a fascinating story that was worthy of being shared with the world. And, with our track record of quality productions, Lutherans, they told us, were the right group to produce it. That weekend proved to be a most effective jump start to reviving the dream I shared with our Lutheran Film Associates trustees. I didn't have to convince them that we should go ahead.

We went to work. Not only did we have our seasoned and faithful team of producer Lothar Wolff (now independent from deRochemont) and freelance screenwriter Allan Sloane, but right on our board was Paul Lammers from CBS television. It was a joy to work with these skilled professionals. Sure, we had some personality issues—artists are given to temperament—but, fortunately, I was able to mediate between and among them. The moments when I felt our unity was threatened all seemed somehow to get resolved—mostly, I know, because each member of our team was a person of integrity. We respected one another. All of the team came to love Bach. Lothar and Allan were, of course, compensated. But Paul's tremendous contribution as director was all *pro bono*. That allowed him to remain as chairman of our LFA board, where he was a natural advocate for our cause. A couple of times the chain-of-command responsibility arose as we faced the need to resolve a dispute—a balking cameraman, for example. "Either he goes or I go" is a phrase I heard several times. Technically, Lammers was my superior as chair of our board, while my role as executive producer gave me clout with the production issues. Such moments were rare, thank God, and we were able to resolve each of them harmoniously.

My decades of curiosity and appreciation for Johann Sebastian Bach certainly paid off for me during the 1970s as our team argued, proposed, rejected, substituted, discovered, and created new scenario sequences. My choices formed the musical menu; what began as a wish list was regularly revised and replaced by another gem that intrigued us.

Lothar was a refugee who fled from Hitler to Denmark before immigrating to the United States. His cultural background, his veteran film-maker's eye, and his understanding of German *Gestalt* were perfect for this project, which unrolled largely in the land where Bach had lived and worked, but which had an international aspect as well. Wolff had lived and worked in Paris for the U.S. Marshall Plan, and he spoke French well. His linguistic skills were a priceless gift to us as he negotiated various arrangements and agreements with artists and institutions where our cameras and sound recorders would be welcomed.

Allan had proved to us with his work on *Martin Luther* that he could absorb an amazing library of information rapidly and thoroughly. He quickly mastered the Bach data and legends. What a marvelous experience to witness such a creative mind at work! One day in a script session he recounted seeing some street musicians playing on the corner of Forty-ninth Street and Fifth Avenue. "I stopped to listen, and—what do you think? They were playing Bach! Why not put them in our film?"

While both Lothar and Allan were Jewish, anyone on the outside might reasonably conclude that both were confirmed Lutherans. They knew our history, theology, practices, and even our politics better than most of my co-religionists. Paul and I were indeed Lutherans; while this could not help but inform our judgments, we made an effort to serve the larger audience so that the resulting film would not be tainted by parochialism.

Paul was one of the main directors for daytime soap operas; at the time of our collaboration, his show was *As the World Turns*. It was during this period that his show morphed from "live" to "recorded." When I was invited to watch Paul direct a show from rehearsal through airing on CBS, I was impressed with his energy as his vision was realized.

This vision was exercised in our regular creative script sessions in Lothar's offices. After these lengthy sessions with Paul, the walls were plastered with notes and signs and sequence possibilities.

I won't forget the session when he came up with the idea for visualizing the music to be sung by the Brooklyn Boys' Choir. I played for our group a recording of the lively duet for alto and soprano from Bach's Cantata no. 78, "Wir Eilen." It was about running to Jesus, and the music was running music. Paul asked, "Why not have these choir boys from Brooklyn filmed running and leaping and skate boarding while we hear them singing this vigorous song?" We played it again, and again, and, sure enough, we could "see" it happening. The choir's conductor was delighted to cooperate. My son Paul spent that day with us on location in Brooklyn's Prospect Park. I was pleased and proud to share my film-making life with him. The resulting scene was a winner!

It was during this preparatory period that we made several scouting trips to Europe—to Bach country itself in communist East Germany (DDR).

I had seen Brian Blessed, the British actor, play the role of Caesar Augustus in *I Claudius*, a popular PBS-from-BBC TV serial drama at that time. It was a good showcase for his versatility. When I saw how the makeup artists aged him during that series, I felt, "That is just what we need for our main Bach character, young and old." We had him do a screen test in costume, and Bach suddenly came alive for us on the screen for the first time.

Brian was a delight to work with. He had been trained as an operatic singer, mostly for its development of breath control that an actor needs, just as a singer does. He was no stranger to music. While we were on location, we had to exercise some patience with him sometimes, but that is normal when dealing with stars. One time in a hotel in Leipzig, we met for breakfast before traveling to our next film site. Brian, a seasoned traveler, had brought his luggage down to the lobby so we could leave soon after the meal. But when he went to fetch his bags, they were gone. The hotel clarified the mystery for us. A tour group leaving our hotel that morning had simply included Brian's luggage with their own. Next stop for them—and Brian's luggage—was Moscow! It took several days before he got it all back.

Another time we were driving on the DDR autobahn from East Berlin to Potsdam for filming at the palace of Frederick the Great. Suddenly a police car was blinking its lights behind us and pulled us over to the side of the highway. *Die Volkspolizei* (*Volpo*, for short) had noticed that we had a West Berlin rental car and decided to check us out. We had to pull out our passports and show our visas. No problem. But wait! Brian did not have his passport with him. *What?* Yes, he had left it in the hotel, one of the most foolish things a Westerner could do in a communist state (or any foreign country, for that matter). Just then, another car arrived. The driver got out and had a private conversation with our policeman. Suddenly, all was well. We were clear to go. It turned out that the new arrival was our shadow. We recognized him from some other location where he had shown up before—we knew him from his party button. He had been ahead of us, and when we hadn't caught up with him, he smelled trouble and came back to find us—and rescue us. Sometimes such political "keepers" actually do keep us from harm.

I had worried that during our filming, the communist government might give us Americans a hard time. This was still during the hard-line days of the Red regime, which didn't collapse until a decade or so later when the Berlin Wall cracked and fell. But the officials couldn't have been more cooperative. To be sure, we had hired crews from their government-operated television, which was most willing to give us the best. Their pride was at stake. Doubtless they had some hope that we would spread the word in the United States that they were technically and artistically up-to-date. They assigned one of their top directors to be our liaison to help us navigate their bureaucracy. One time he invited Lothar, Paul, Brian, and me to his home for dinner. I didn't fail to note that their television was carrying a West Berlin program.

The DDR officials wanted to help us find the best locations. We knew that Bach had served Prince Leopold at Köthen, and we wanted to film in his royal castle. They explained that, while the old castle was still standing, it had been renovated since Bach's time during the Romantic period and therefore would not look like an authentic Baroque location. So we were given a substitute that had been restored to match the early 1700s. It was a perfect setting (lots of mirrors) in which to film the Prince's guests dancing a Bach minuet, with the Maestro himself at the harpsichord, surrounded by a small orchestra.

And similarly we were invited to Frederick the Great's castle at Potsdam. It was now a museum; our crew all had to wear special slippers (except for Brian as Bach, of course) so as not to damage the fancy parquet floors. We also had to ration our hot film lights and turn them off at intervals in order to protect the precious original paintings on the walls.

Our scenario had several sequences calling for authentic pipe organs of Bach's period. One in particular included Bach's testing of an organ built by his friend Gottfried Silbermann. We were given the choice of three or four beautifully restored Silbermann instruments, and we used them all for various settings.

Most importantly, perhaps, we had entrée to the two famous buildings in Leipzig that appear today virtually as they did in Bach's time—the City Hall and the St. Thomas Church just down the street from it.

In our filming we weren't limited to East Germany. After all, we were making a film about Bach's music, not just his career. Because Bach's music has become an international treasure, we also filmed scenes in Paris and London. Back home in the United States we filmed in Minnesota, Iowa, Montana, and Maryland, as well as Washington, D.C. and New York City.

Finally we had all our shooting done. Then began the post-production process. That's always when I am the most impatient. But our film editor, Morrie Roizman, was fantastic in making the footage sing! At one time with material we had shot abroad—a well-known Bach fugue played by a German organist—we decided that we had to abridge it for purposes of time. Where best to make the cuts? That time I called upon the High Priestess of Bach, Rosalyn Tureck herself, to help us in the post-production process. She came to our studio to listen to the various fugue entries and watch the organist's fingers. She then figured out for us the exact points where we could match A with B without jolting any listening musicians, thereby saving several precious minutes for us.

We had a wonderful sequence filmed at Jacob's Pillow, the summer dance site in Massachusetts. Flamenco dancer Theo Morca had created a brilliant sequence to the music of Bach's *Toccata and Fugue in D Minor*, on a recording by E. Power Biggs, playing not the organ but a pedal harpsichord. Weeks later, back in the editing suite, we discovered to our dismay that the sound of his clacking castanets and his clicking toes was garbled against a fuzzy harpsichord background. We had to summon Morca back to Manhattan. In a studio I directed his dancing sequence, recording a cleaner sound as he watched himself dancing on a screen to the same music. This time we were able to get it properly recorded, mixed, and dubbed over the original sound track.

So many rich experiences, so many fond memories, of brilliant musicians performing for us! Some of them required take after take until they (and we) were satisfied. In Madame Tureck's own montage, which included seamless sections of the same piece played seriatim on a clavichord, harpsichord, piano, and electronic keyboard, she herself recorded twenty-three takes on the electronic keyboard before she was satisfied with the result. They all sounded good to me.

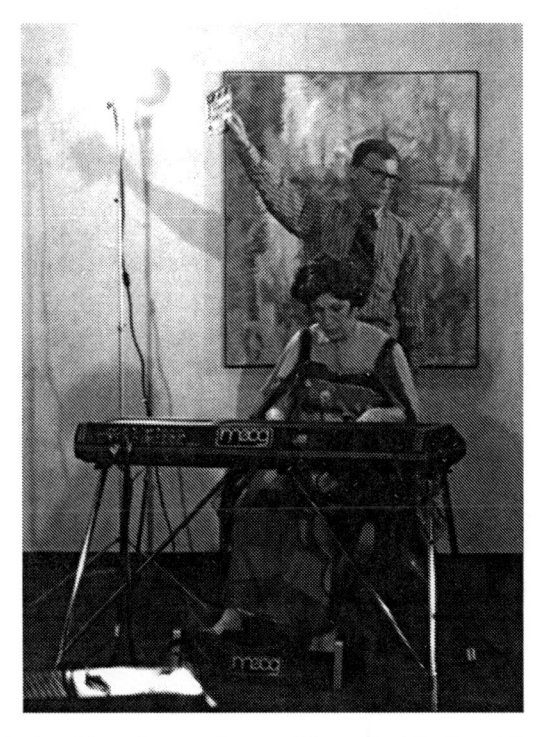

Madam Tureck recording on Moog for *The Joy of Bach*

At last we were ready for launching our *opus magnus*. We expected that it might only be slotted on the PBS system, since the commercial networks liked to do their own productions. We had a ninety-minute program, and when PBS saw it, they loved it. But their condition for accepting *The Joy of Bach* was that it could be only a one-hour show. How painful it was to cut out an entire half hour! WQED in Pittsburgh, our entry station, agreed to trim it to size for us. I dreaded the loss of some favorite scenes but have to agree that they made good choices, and I could still be proud of the result. PBS programmed it at Christmas. That seemed strange to me, but they pursued that seasonal idea and asked me, "Doesn't the show have some Christmas angle?" I could only come up with the fact that there were two scenes featuring music from the Christmas Oratorio—both quite short sequences, to be sure—but that was enough for them. Not only did it run in early December, but they liked it well enough to run it at the same annual holiday three more years in a row.

For me, a film lover and a Bach lover, *Joy* became the crowning jewel of my "magic" moviemaking career.

13 Popcorn & Parable

I was quite taken aback one time in the mid-1960s when a publicist working for deRochemont Productions (within whose Manhattan office suite I was then situated) said to me upon hearing my views on a movie, "But you're not a critic!"

Maybe he was right. Of course I didn't write for a top newspaper or widely circulated publication. But I did do film reviews. I had some of them published in our church periodicals, but mostly they were heard on radio on my syndicated weekly show *Cinema Sound,* describing and depicting contemporary Hollywood movies. Maybe the term "critic" should be applied only to the top strata of reviewers. I considered myself a journalist. And a filmmaker. And a broadcaster. And a publicist, too, for that matter. His words did resonate uncomfortably with me, however, and thereafter I took care not to identify myself as a critic, even though others might be generous and apply the term to me.

In my work I enjoyed ecumenical cooperation within the Broadcasting and Film Commission of the National Council of Churches (NCC), which included most mainline Protestant and Orthodox denominations. I was our Lutheran representative on that BFC board. I wrote reviews for their publication, *Film Information,* about current cinema. That was ticket enough to gain access to the screenings. I developed a system for taking notes in the dark while watching the screen and hoping that I could later decipher what the scribbles meant.

Later, when I was more seasoned and was within the critics' crowd at private screenings, attending film festivals such as those in Montreal, Berlin, Venice, and Cannes, I told myself I had every right to think of myself—and, when appropriate, even identify myself—as a critic.

One reason for wanting to review films was my conviction that movies—similar to popular fiction—offered insights into the human condition that could help individuals better understand their own situation. I like to think that a story that conveys humanity's issues, traumas, successes, failures, fears, and triumphs can be a kind of case study for discussion groups—or for individuals to think and converse about. What would you do in that situation? What are the moral and ethical themes in the work? Whenever possible I would lift up those themes in movies. With Roger Kahle I wrote a book that we called *Popcorn and Parable*. Films can be parables almost in the biblical sense—stories like Jesus told that engage one and invite the person to think of implications with which the viewer might identify.

The undercurrent of meaning in the story was what we were trying to help people discover. Some of us who had communication portfolios in national church organizations were urging our constituents to do more than look at movies for escapist entertainment. They could also look at movies to see something of themselves, because movies reveal how we live, move, and have our being.

The moral and spiritual aspect of cinema was the basis of the religion department course I taught for three semesters at Adelphi University, near me in Garden City on Long Island. It was also the basis for a cable television program that I produced and hosted for several years, called *VISN on Film*. Though I still love movies, I don't keep up with them any more. I wish I did.

Hollywood, of course, is not interested in educating and evangelizing movie-goers. Many in filmdom are primarily interested in making money. We found, nonetheless, that most film artists covet support—rather than criticism—from churches, as long as do-gooders don't censor their efforts or stand in the way of gaining big box office receipts. The National Council of Churches, together with the Roman Catholic national film office, formed a steering committee to relate to the film industry. Our goal was not to fight Hollywood for its questionable films, but rather commend filmmakers for their quality movies and urge more development of substantial stories with some strong moral and ethical motifs. Our premise was that writers, producers, and directors of integrity who have uplifting values are eager to have these ideals reflected in their work, provided they can still tell a good story and not be didactic in the process.

We established a connection with the Motion Picture Association of America (MPAA). Its president for many years was Jack Valenti, whose earlier celebrity status was as an assistant to President Lyndon Johnson. When Valenti and his staff invited us to their offices to discuss various concerns, we considered these issues important from the churches' side, and they wanted understanding from us. They also needed our support for the film rating system that was being launched, and we were glad to help in evaluating it.

Some of our meetings were at their headquarters in Washington, D.C., where they had a large screening room, and others were in Hollywood. The annual sessions, however, were on Sixth Avenue in New York City, as they usually included leaders of the theater owners association. At one of those Big

Apple sessions, I was fascinated by a fellow sitting across the table from me. He had a familiar face. Who was it? Someone famous, I thought. Then when Valenti asked him a question and used the name "Louis," his name suddenly came to me: Louis Nizer. "One of the most celebrated trial lawyers in the country" according to the *New York Times*, he was there as legal counsel to MPAA.

When the meeting adjourned, Nizer called me over to him and tore a page off his yellow pad. There was a sketch of me! While participating in the discussion he had been busy with his pencil, drawing my bearded face. He inscribed it "Louis Nizer—1/5/72" and gave it to me. Years later I was fascinated to read in a feature article in the *New York Times* that this sketch represented a marvelous habit of this Renaissance man:

> A positively obsessive sketcher, he has done caricatures of judges, witnesses, juries and other lawyers while arguing a host of sensational lawsuits, many involving actors, actresses and writers. Nizer explained, "I am able to concentrate on what's being said while drawing."

Our ecumenical group launched an annual film award program. We would choose the top movies of the year in each new January, and then a small group of us as judges would get together at special screenings to share and compare our reviews and discuss the merits and demerits of each. It was a fascinating process. We always came out with a consensus and made a big deal out of our winner. We would have a banquet or large luncheon and invite the producer or director or stars. Hollywood's notables welcomed this kind of affirmation. Soon the major TV networks took turns offering us time for presenting our awards on the air. After all, they could get film personalities and stars on their show, and film clips could be shown. On several occasions I represented our committee on behalf of the Protestant/Orthodox community. Sometimes we would have a network news person like Hugh Downs or Charles Kuralt moderating the telecast.

I originated a weekly radio program that was distributed by syndication to hundreds of radio stations. I gave it the title *Cinema Sound*, and the National Council of Churches and the Episcopal Church joined us Lutherans as producers for this film review program. We set goals and deadlines for my writing and recording reviews. We offered stations the choice of two formats: one, a sixty-second spot, and the other, a four-minute segment. I wrote the longer one first since that was the easiest. Boiling it down to one minute was often the most difficult, but it proved to be a very good exercise for me as a writer. One tries to give listeners in such reviews a reason for deciding whether the film being described would be of interest to them and whether it would be worthwhile for them to see. I liked to pick films to review that had relevance, something to say, that could be considered parables. It is easiest to pan a film and rip it apart. Sometimes that was necessary if a popular film in my estimation was simply sophisticated garbage. But most films that sincerely try to reflect life honestly often have content that could carry meaning to listeners and viewers.

The other day I found some dusty boxes in an attic storeroom in my house and pulled them out. There were hundreds of scripts of film reviews that continued through the 1970s and deep into the 1980s. And, because these had been recorded for radio, I also had boxes of audio tape cassettes. So I listened to some of them and perused a number of the script pages. I had, of course, forgotten even seeing or reviewing many of them.

I picked up one script page that carried a review of one of the most sensitive and profound films of the early 1980s. It was *Tender Mercies*, directed by Australian Bruce Beresford, but the story was classic Americana. I can still visualize some of the touching scenes.

The story by Horton Foote depicts the rebuilding of a life through new-found relationships. Robert Duvall, in what must be an Academy Award-winning acting accomplishment, plays a country-western singer on the skids. [Note: Duvall did get the Oscar!] There's not a wasted moment or gesture or word; we believe him, we accept him. Tess Harper is the war widow who takes him in and marries him. Her ten-year old son, who has never seen his own father, learns to love him also. The boy, Allan Hubbard in his first role, is almost perfect.

Religion—Southern Baptist variety—is important in *Tender Mercies*. Even that title comes from the words of a real prayer, honestly prayed. A worship service is included with reverence and respect and a touch of natural humor. We are not surprised, but are fascinated, when the boy is baptized by total immersion. But we are surprised and delighted when the repenting singer is next. This prepares us for tragedy and for the healing that comes.

Some years earlier I had published an article asking "Why don't characters in movies ever pray?" Admittedly, seeing or hearing movie characters in prayer had been rare, and still is. But I found it to be true that when the prayers are intrinsic to the plot, they can be most revealing and highly dramatic as well. A psychiatrist friend once told me, "If you really want to know a person, listen (if you can) to his prayers." That question about prayer on the screen struck a nerve with the film industry, it seems, for *Variety*, the so-called bible of moviemaking, spread out my critique of Hollywood in one of its editions, and I got calls from other media asking about it. *Tender Mercies* was a gratifying exception.

During the height of my reviewing, I would sometimes take on other issues that had some moral relevance. Language was one of these. There was a time when movies were almost sanitized. When Clark Gable used the word "damn" in the classic 1939 Civil War movie *Gone With the Wind*, it made news! Because so much had changed forty years later, I wrote a piece that called on the movie industry to "clean up your sound tracks!" Some ridiculed me for being too pious and puritanical, but others agreed because they also had found gratuitous foul talk offensive. Language, as well as sex, nudity, and violence, can mostly be judged on the basis of how intrinsic these elements are to the integrity of the story and its context. Most moviegoers today can decide whether or not an R rating—often labeled for language—will discourage them from choosing a particular film.

Some in the religious communities also blasted me for my position on other controversial movies. For example, when Martin Scorcese filmed the Kazantzakis story *The Last Temptation of Christ,* it was highly volatile even before its release. I was invited to a private, ticket-only, screening in Manhattan. As soon as I arrived, I sensed that there was electricity in the crowd outside the preview theater. Security was tight and there were protest signs. I saw the film and agreed that some scenes seemed to cross the line into questionable territory. But I also knew that the Greek author sincerely wanted to pose the question about Jesus—was he really and truly human, a man, or was he, as God's son, not really human but sinless and divine? Could he be tempted? The Bible is specific about the fact that he was indeed tempted. Kazantzakis used the literary technique of a dream or hallucination fantasy to underscore the humanity of Jesus—suggesting that in the dream he yields to the temptation and is married, with sexual congress and children following. But the delirium scenario illustrated temptation while Jesus was on the cross. It was the last temptation in this story; clearly the movie shows that Jesus resisted it. Not everybody would buy the literary license of such a dream sequence. But I felt it was a powerful way to help people struggle with the enigma of the God-Man Jesus presented in the New Testament.

CNN invited me to debate the issue live with a stern critic of the *The Last Temptation of Christ.* It was one of those memorable challenges I lived through (and learned from) during my movie reviewing days. I discovered that when I made some comment that appeared a bit outrageous, the media picked it up, and I had invitations to radio and TV talk shows. I hasten to add, that's not why I wrote what I wrote. Most of what I had written and published didn't create any ripples.

The Jesus story has been handled or mishandled by various filmmakers over the years. *Jesus of Montreal*, which never made it big in cinema release, is one of the most satisfying of these attempts because it is the most intimately troubling. The viewer is drawn into the story's radical claims, sensing its dangers, its injustice, while the drama teases and feelings flow. How different from the usual passion plays on film (or on stage) that only allow the spectator to look *at* the action while remaining empathetically detached from it. The director Denys Arcand, who also plays the title role, finds a dramatically engaging way to show the radical side of the Christ who is an offense to the religious and civil establishment. He updates—as if it's happening today—the calling of the disciples, Jesus' baptism, the chasing of the money lenders from the temple, the arrest and trial and death of Jesus, and the impact on his followers.

The *Revolt of Job*, a Hungarian film released in the United States in 1984, may still be one of the most profoundly religious films ever made. A pious Jewish couple, after seven of their own children have died, adopt a blond Christian boy about eight years old to raise as their own during World War II. They have a keen premonition of tragedy ahead—the Nazis have already taken over Hungary—and this couple wants to fulfill parental obligations in obedience to God. How to do this and still respect the boy's Christian heritage leads to a wonderful story, beautifully filmed. The peasant farmer's name is Job. When his wife scolds him for yielding to the sin of despair, the biblical allusion is permitted an explicit moment. When, near the end of the movie, a funeral procession of horse-drawn carts carries the Jews away like some bad dream of a Holocaust parade, the lad is bereft of all but his foster father's instructions to search for the Messiah. That final scene of *The Revolt of Job* becomes a primal parable of hope amidst despair. It remains before our eyes as a kind of rare cinematic phylactery.

There are thousands of film stories that can stimulate reflection, all the way from today's sleepers to yesterday's classics. Either in a theater, where we can participate in a collective experience of flickering action and mood mirrored from a huge screen, or in the solitude of our own home with the bouncing images on the video screen, what we see reflected is illusion. But the light carries meaning. It shows us symbols. It speaks to us in visual metaphors. It can reflect back to us something of ourselves.

Forty years ago near the end of our book *Popcorn and Parable*, Kahle and I wrote:

> Films, like parables, are illustrations of life. We can discount the objective information conveyed through a film. We can get facts, data, statistics in other ways. Any good illustration is dramatic and essentially must have a point and must indeed point to some larger premise or truth. Mature and concerned persons desperately need to look at "slices of life" in order to see into themselves, and films can provide this. Television helps us see outwardly—the very name means "seeing at a distance"—but cinema helps us see inwardly.

14 Writing Therapy

I have been writing all my life but only now, in retirement, do I claim to be a writer. Before this stage, writing was mostly functional. I composed broadcast scripts, news releases, articles, and even some books. But it was usually a means to an end. Most often a part of my job.

What delight, then, to finally discover that writing could become recreation, something that I could do quite easily, producing what I felt was respectable as prose, or even poetry. But only when I caught on that writing-for-the-sake-of-writing was possible—I wasn't just wasting time—did it dawn on me that this might actually be a calling. This late in life? Sure, I wanted to keep busy and needed to. Because writing captivated me, I realized I was compelled to write. I began to think of myself as a *writer*! I have always put writers on a pedestal. What about humility? I hear my friends, maybe even my family, pitching in with "Humility be damned! Do it! Keep doing it! Think whatever you want to think!"

Another way to put it is that I have a need to speak out, to communicate, to share. Okay. That sounds reasonable, acceptable, supportable. But, in all honesty, I write because I love to write.

For me it is therapy. I spend a couple of hours allowing my fingers on the computer keyboard to lead me on in speed writing—getting the ideas and the words out and fixing them later on. It's like other creative activities that are hindered by one's applying preventive self-censorship. Edit by all means. But let it out first. We have this wonderful tool that allows us to change, move stuff around, and cut and paste without scissors or glue.

I give thanks that I took those courses in high school where I learned touch typing long before computers were ever dreamed of. My life has been different because of that early typing skill. In every aspect of my career, I found that typing was my tool for expressing words. I call it "thinking through my fingers." I now realize that this has been of inestimable value to me. And personally, it saves me from the embarrassment of having to read my handwriting!

I never studied the art of creating poems. Only now in retirement have I been catching up and absorbing a lot of wonderful word paintings. But I have been experimenting. I have been helped by reading about writing, and I have begun to parse the verses and learn from them. I have found that it is no accident that the best lyrics for songs are quality poems in their own right.

Most of all I find that trying to create poems to satisfy myself—not some expert or critic—is therapeutically stimulating. I feel free somehow. I love to sketch out descriptive sounds of choice words and let them sing for me. I sense that they should read well aloud. I also am quite aware that, like biblical psalms as poetry, thematic and emotion-and-action-packed verses are often puzzles that on the surface seem to make little sense. So far I feel constricted by all that freedom, even though I respect it and even covet the ability to lay out these mysterious words and phrases. A little alliteration and rhyme are okay, but it is easy to slip into language that is trite or corny. Maybe I should take some lessons. But the best way to learn to write poetry, according to one of our recent Poet Laureates, is to *read* poetry.

Having said that and given my apologia, I am sharing herewith some poems I have created—writing them and setting them out on these pages, just for the joy of doing it.

Pear Tree Divided

Half of it still stands there swinging in the breeze
Seeming almost to shiver in the autumn chill
Reluctant to change her coat from green to gold
Knowing the reckoning day will surely come.

My Bradford Pear's pain remained
When its better half split that day
That deciding day
When a devilish dancing breeze
Became a whip-lash storm
Carrying unexpected strength
Cleaving crazily with a maelstrom of might
Cracking the left from the right
Splitting the right from the left
Dividing my tall, proud pear tree
Lovely leafy limbs in nurtured union.

I trembled to hear it, to see it falling
I wept to view its fractured frame.

Time heals as it tends to do in my life
I saw tree surgeons saw and seal and separate
The newly challenged limbs lifted their arms again
To meet the sun the moon the snow the rain
Forgetting the panic forgetting the pain,
As if deciding *What now? What's left to gain?*

I waited the winter
Watching the leafless skeleton
Swinging in the icy wind.

Then the answer came
When nature sprang awake
White flowers peeked out
Cautious green began to grow
Crippled boughs soon looked to the sun
Offering a gift of gratitude—fresh shade
And as if there were no past stain nor strain
Began again to stand proudly there
Swinging in the breeze.

Robert E. A. Lee [2004]

Genetic Gratitude

It returns most gently assertive
My awareness of the gift
Poring through old photos.

Who are these people with their puzzled frowns
Or caught in the midst of a laugh
Or snapped in awkward poses
Grinning, mugging into the archival lens?

Why, they are my people!
They are me—father mother uncles aunts
And of course brother and sisters
I pause to see symbolic similarities
I study especially our family sisterhood.

Strong women standing tall
Parental posture modeled and proclaimed
Stand up straight, slouch not!
Voice of the matriarch instructing
Be proud, not ashamed, of who you are.

Courage came gifted to the sorority she mothered
She was truly proud of her quintet
A secret seldom if ever shared aloud
She bequeathed (to all but her first)
The art of surviving long in life
Vital and vigorous into eighth and ninth decades
She willed a stalwart spine morally resolute
And into the motivational bloodline of her offspring
Her love of learning came DNA-transfused.

These strong-willed capable devoted daughters
Inherited as well generous traits
Traced from our father's fun and cozy warmth
Attributes emerging in my sisters' own living replication
Remembered when nostalgic thoughts reach back
To hear his stories still stirring us
His songs still singing to us.

I too feel from the mystic photos
The resonance of life evoked from these albums
Recall faces recognize voices
Hum tunes and replay memory reels
I was nourished from childhood
Under the watchful umbrella of sisters.

Robert E. A. Lee [2004]

Commuter's Sound Track

I walked to my train this morning
Along a busy sound track.

The sound level of hum and hiss
Was punctuated by swishing slip streams
From passing cars.

The inner turmoil of heated engines
Surfaced in sighs groans
Coughs sneezes.
Angry trucks licked the pavement
Snorting and wheezing
At us fellow travelers.

A captive hound in parked sedan
Pleaded for his master's voice.

The agitated wind
Added its own decibel dirge
To merge with the morning's surface noise.

From above
A prompt intruded
I looked up seeking its sound source
There up high in a guard-duty tree
A bird unseen called to me
Claiming and proclaiming
His primal song
Above earth-bound traffic.

Robert E. A. Lee [1982]

In the Tempo of Time

Where did April go?
I wasn't ready even when it came
Maybe looking the other way
Lost in the winds and Ides of March
The world tells me this April is gone forever.

April previewed May before escaping
Sunny blue skies green leaves sprouting
Blossoms rejoicing at their homecoming.

Where were the April showers?
Are the seasons out of sync
Skewed by thawing arctic ice?

April didn't even hesitate
No sentimental goodbye
Its moments retreated as unremembered breaths
Life's momentum accelerating through my decades
Yet ticking in tempo with billions of spent heartbeats.

We mourn the passing days years
Collective lives slipping by
Into some cosmic memory dust
I beg first to snatch and archive
Random reflections in any open brain cells.

April left us to make room for May
Each dawn bringing its promise of new life
Coming into the spring air of delight
One more renewal one more chance one more gift
From the one Gift Giver who alone can open the door
And invite us into tomorrow.

Robert E. A. Lee [2006]

Sunset

The maples are a little late this year
Most neighbor trees have already undressed
I was seasonally certain my maples' cue would come.

Raining it was when I first caught the change
Drooping drenched green destined for crimson
What glory in damp foliage?
My maples will redeem themselves.

Today God's sun announced show and tell
Brilliant sun-dried copper gold yellow red.
Worth a November celebration.

I wait for dusk to descend
When the solar light slips below my western view
Anticipating its precious prelude to sunset
Low-slanting rays flood leafy jewels
Dancing light unfolding into twilight.

Sunset Maple aptly named
Deserving front-lawn status
While Japanese maples seem far away
In their back-yard grove.

Sunset comes in each life's calendar
Late afternoon glow is sensed and seen
Felt and perhaps even feared.

Yet incredible color splashing against autumn clouds
Bespeaks a promise proffered by our rotating globe
Carrying you me and all in this real world
Not west to the sunset
Rather as each new morning attests
Toward the sunrise.

Robert E. A. Lee [2004]

15 God's Mysterious Gift

I had not thought much about fatherhood in anticipating a role for myself in life. I was too busy growing up. Too busy trying to find myself and my role in World War II. And adding the wondrous merger of lives that was my marriage to Elaine. I knew parenthood normally came with the package, but it remained a distant possibility sometime in the future.

I wasn't a plotter and planner at that stage of my life. Wartime had put a kind of spell on us. We didn't dare plan or think too specifically about what the future would be like. I had vague dreams about a home for the two of us with a piano and a fireplace and cozy togetherness. The sound of babies and more babies had not yet been heard.

But that changed. And how it changed! Suddenly there I was, not yet a twenty-five-year-old, holding baby Peggy, our first-born. It was an inscrutable miracle then and, even after six kids, is still miraculous: that these living personalities—growing and developing and giving and receiving—were born to us, Elaine and Bob, mother and father. Just as she—wife, lover, friend, companion—was clearly God's gift to me, and I to her, so our children were gifted to us by God. A mystery then and always—the very fact of life. The glorious secret we cherished was that our two lives had morphed into one. Since we first experienced the reality of oneness when I returned from duty in the Pacific after V-J Day, neither of us ever just took it for granted. Once the war was mercifully behind us, our life was again changed. Mother. Father. Then the multiplication parade began: 1946 Peg, 1947 Barbara, 1951 Sigrid, 1953 Richard, 1955 Sylvia, and 1959 Paul. Blessings, each and all.

Why did this seem mysterious? Normal, rather, the world would tell us. We insisted, however, that to us had been given a sextet of miracles. Without our specifically applying for it, God had commissioned us to bear, raise, love, nurture, and then set free these fresh new human beings. Yes, they carried in their DNA a long heritage from Norse forebears from each family—farmers, professors, entrepreneurs, clergy, musicians, teachers, and maybe even a scoundrel or two. We both knew well, without having to be told, that we had an irrevocable moral pact with our Creator to accept responsibility for these new beings. In the sacramental ritual of baptism, God's divine commitment was promised as a gift of the Holy Spirit to accompany each child through life. Enabling, enlightening, guiding, comforting. We had witnesses. Sponsors. Talk about mystery!

Over my life span of fatherhood, I have learned that responsibility means safeguarding; it means preparing tender fledglings to "keep their airspeed" when they fly out of the nest; and it means teaching, training, urging on, and sometimes holding back. It means giving our children the sustenance for living and the tools and wherewithal for meeting daily challenges. I have the satisfaction at this point in my life that in most instances our kids had what they needed. So many times along the way, I would ache with desire to give them so much more. My heart was generous, but my purse could not be. I got burned once when I promised my daughter that she would go to Europe before college. Good intentions can't be gift-wrapped.

I also saw my paternal role as sharing happy times with our children. We didn't really try to keep up with the neighbors. The kind of holiday jaunts they enjoyed we couldn't afford. However, our large family had many genuine good times. From a father's memory, the trips across the country to visit our relatives in Minnesota, Iowa, and Wisconsin, are special. And we did get in some weeks in lakeside cabins. Most of our children remember waiting, as we rolled along, for the moment we were to enter each tunnel along the Pennsylvania Turnpike in order to make the most of the little mechanical sparklers they had along to celebrate the dark passage. Who else can boast of that bit of travel entertainment trivia?

It was often on trips I took with each of our kids separately that I felt closest to them. Just the two of us. Most of the time Elaine hauled each of them around on Long Island for their various appointments and lessons and school activities. But sometimes I had that one-to-one chance also. For example, I took Sylvia to Oberlin in Ohio for her freshman year. I remember the exhilaration of our singing together along the turnpike, enjoying the luxury of a motel for the one night en route, and, finally, exploring that fascinating campus together. I found myself buoyed by her fresh enthusiasm for her new discoveries ahead. I knew music would be a priority for her, and later I was proud to be at Lincoln Center and to hear her featured in a quartet in the famed Oberlin choir singing part of a Beethoven mass.

Paul and I rode in our orange Camaro the fifty miles back and forth to the university at Stony Brook out on Long Island when he would come home for the weekend. Buying that sporty car was our response to his wishes more than our own. He seemed to enjoy driving it, but one time after fetching Elaine and me at JFK, he was stopped by a police patrol car with blinking red lights and scolded—and maybe ticketed?—for exceeding the speed limit in Lynbrook. We didn't chastise him. We didn't need to.

Paul and Sylvia's departure for higher education left us parents with an empty nest at long last. Our first such goodbye had been about a dozen years earlier when we left Peg at Brandt Hall at Luther College. I had driven out halfway across the nation with all the family except Elaine. It was a different trip without her, but it was also a different return without our oldest daughter, the first one of the sextet to fly away. My choked up emotion left my eyes teary as we drove away from that Iowa campus. I remember being impressed then with how Barbara spontaneously moved with grace into the new role as our family's first lieutenant. She just assumed the authority to be in charge, and the others fell in line with no evident objection. I didn't orchestrate that.

Peg relished her college years. I still have some of her college art work hanging on my walls. Homecoming at Luther College four years later marked the twenty-fifth anniversary of my graduation. Not only was I the main speaker at the alumni dinner where I was honored with a Distinguished Alumni Award, but later that same night—as a complete surprise to Elaine and me—Peg was crowned as Campus Queen in an impressive ceremony. How proud this dad was.

Peg generates paternal pride often with her enviable artistic talent. I love it when I can visit her studio and she shows me the evidence of her creativity. And she has been generous about providing me with sketches or brochures I wanted for my work. I'm grateful that her artist husband Sherwin, a graphics designer, also contributes creative ideas. Most especially I appreciate the countless years of collaboration on the design of our annual Christmas card. Peg has a natural flair for decorating a page in a way that conveys the message and, at the same time, reflects her (and my) taste.

Peg is the expert I consult when I need some re-decorating help. Her professional career is interior design. Whether it's a new bathroom or a carpet or the color of a wall, she pleases her dad with her generous ideas. Most of the artwork in the house reflects her artistic integrity as well.

She has her mother's flair for dressing smartly. It's not just the apparel she chooses but more often the way she wears a scarf, her striking use of color in her wardrobe, and the upbeat carriage I am proud to notice as she comes striding down Wall Street to meet me for lunch in Manhattan.

She is a busy person but has been setting aside one evening a week, usually Wednesday, to come out on the train to Baldwin to have dinner with me and to stay overnight. A great treat for her old man!

The frequent singing within our family has left me with precious memory sounds that I hear again as I re-read my journal.

Peg and Barbara were home with us—we were singing hymns—I was at the piano and both of my daughters were sitting with Elaine on the couch, one on each side supporting her with their arms and their songs. What a blessing music can be when our soul needs something and we feel ready to let go of our tension from the day.

Even before she could talk, Peggy would hum tunes as she played with the kitchen pots and pans, preferring them to store-bought toys. Now with her own grandchildren she will create cute little dolls and handmade play material out of whatever elements are close at hand—rocks, stones, boxes, clay, flowers. An interesting contrast to the upscale commercial designs that she developed with her firm's client, American Girl.

Barbara was born in Montana during the year we lived there. That night there was a minor earthquake registered. Elaine saw a hanging light in her hospital room swaying, apparently from that modest event that I knew nothing of until the next morning. Barb's advent into our family allowed us to celebrate two daughters. And we knew they would be close, inasmuch as they were only fourteen months apart. They have continued to be close as the senior siblings of the Lee clan. I have often quoted Barbara's poignant question, *Why didn't you have me borned first?*

Violent as the elements were as she was ushered into the world, Barbara's mien has always been calm, collected, warm, and sensible. I have never ever known her to lose her temper, unlike almost everyone else in our family. Her sense of responsibility to help others comes naturally to her. It seems she can never do enough for us, but always she has exceeded our expectations.

Her photos impress me. They are more artistic than ordinary pictures, particularly the nature studies and still-lifes. Her creative talent extends to her work with fabrics, including quilting. I am warmed by the winter scarf she knit for me.

I have enjoyed Barbara's attention and assistance to me as a widower in my retirement that is marked by a writing priority. She inherited Elaine's skill with words and their appropriate use. She spent over three decades in the public schools, first as a French teacher and then a language supervisor. She not only manages my editorial needs (we wrestle with a word or phrase until we come to agreement), but manages my financial needs as well. She is a natural mother, even though she and Eric have no kids of their own. She fusses over me and also over her Aunt Louise. And Barbara is a "mother" as well to many nieces and nephews and their children.

Elaine and I were prudent enough not to try to micromanage the romantic adventures of our progeny. They felt they had our support for their decisions, even though we may privately have been dubious in some cases. When Barbara phoned us from college that she was engaged and wanted to marry Eric, she caught us off guard. It was our first encounter with one of our own crossing into the marital landscape. She was young, perhaps too young, we thought. She had finished only two years at St. Olaf, but Eric was graduating. Later Barbara not only earned her B.A. degree, but added an M.A. as well. Her wedding was the first in our family and became a landmark in our lives—and hers, of course. That happy marriage has lasted over forty years—a tribute, indeed, to their love and dedication and a source of joy for me.

In many ways Sigrid is the liveliest and most ebullient of our flock. She has a great capacity for celebration and has been most prone to flirting with danger. When we visited her at Indiana University, I may have raised my eyebrows at her bohemian living quarters. But she seemed content. The setting seemed to fit her bent as a product of the counter-cultural phenomenon. It was there that she became challenged to pursue music professionally. While it disappointed Elaine and me that she quit Indiana before getting her bachelor's degree, her move to continue music education overseas at the Basel, Switzerland Schola Cantorum was nevertheless progress. It provided her career with an important building block.

Both of us parents were indeed proud to see and hear Sigrid performing ancient Christmas music on a New England tour with the Boston Camerata. She is our "show-case" family musician. Her father is rewarded whenever he thinks back to hearing her perform early music in Europe and on TV from Paris and Canada. She modulated from performance into recorded music production and discovered that she had talents both as an artistic supervisor and a digital editor. She inherited her mother's excellent ear. I was impressed by her efficiency and multilingual diplomacy in directing CD recording sessions on location in ancient churches and in her own studio near Pisa.

Sigrid troubled me and Elaine by her marital adventures that conflicted with our values and moral and spiritual convictions. It was a blow to our Lutheran pride when she converted to Judaism and married Jay at a Jewish wedding. He was a fellow American musician she met at the Schola. That marriage didn't last, nor did her conversion. But from it came a lovely granddaughter, Nina, who now lives in Paris and is following this grandfather's career role in film production.

Eight of us flew over to Italy together to Sigrid's next wedding to Francis, an Italian lutenist, with whom we never really bonded, mostly because we spoke no Italian, and he no English. With Roberto, her present partner, she has enjoyed almost twenty years of domestic (and professional) harmony. When visiting there, we so wished that we could speak Italian.

Sigrid has made many whirlwind visits home from France and Italy. Elaine and Sigrid had to work through their tensions, which may have been exacerbated by the fact that they were so much alike. Near the end of Elaine's life, they were able to enjoy a beautiful rapprochement.

Sigrid showered Elaine with love and attention. She took her out for forty-five minutes one day for some fresh air, pushing her wheelchair down the street and through the park. They both enjoyed it, although it proved to be somewhat colder than they expected. I was glad I had given them an afghan to put over Elaine's legs. Sigrid left this afternoon. It was a tearful goodbye for her with Elaine, although Elaine didn't break down emotionally as Sigrid did; Sigrid could not stem the tears. We exchanged loving words that I will long remember.

Richard seemed philosophical even as a child. When I put him to bed at night he asked me to lie down with him to just talk. His ideas flowed, many of them related to his mental construct of his own government with its leader (himself as president or maybe dictator) and a constitution that he developed. It was all part of his fantasy life, informed by his social studies class at Junior High School. He would put names on a chart and would design organizational tables for the unicameral government that he intended to serve his purposes as a great leader.

This was the turning point in Richard's becoming a student. Before that, he found school entertaining at best. But after that he pursued study aggressively, through a B.A. with math and philosophy majors and a Ph.D. at Stanford. When I sat in on one of Richard's philosophy classes at the University of Arkansas I found out that what I had expected and assumed, that he is an excellent teacher. His gift is the rapport he establishes with his students, sharing his wisdom of and about thought. I chide him frequently about his self-confessed procrastination. I do feel he should write more for publication, and he agrees. I have concluded that my nudging him isn't the answer.

Rich's wife Jeannie accompanies singers and instrumentalists for auditions and recitals. She organizes and directs the music for theatrical productions. Richard has music as his avocation. His musical taste includes the extremes of Gregorian chant and worship of the Beatles.

One time when Rich was in grade school, I was chagrined when a policeman rang our doorbell. I didn't invite him in to join my mother and other relatives visiting from the Midwest but went outside. Richard and his friend Cliff were sitting meekly in the patrol car, its red lights blinking frighteningly. The two young boys had apparently been apprehended in the midst of some mischief in a parking lot behind a row of Baldwin stores. I thanked the cop and told him that I would deal with my son. Rich and I went inside, both of us wearing forced smiles.

When Richard was about twelve, he and I took a transcontinental flight to Hollywood on some film business. The amenities that air travel offered in those days are now mostly missing from coach service. We had a fancy meal, complete with cloth napkins and silver tableware, delivered to the tray at our seats. In those innocent days the tray included a small pack of three or four cigarettes. Unthinkable today! As a smoker then, I welcomed it, and, because my son was soon to "grow up," I invited him to have one of the smokes. He seemed pleased to enjoy it in the presence of his father, a fellow sinner. I am relieved that he never became a smoker.

Sylvia always introduced herself to our guests as "number five." She arrived in 1955, a year after we had moved our busy household to Long Island. Her grandfather C.G. Naeseth, who had only recently retired from the ministry, was visiting us in Baldwin, since Elaine's mother had died the year before. While awaiting the birth of the new baby, C.G. seemed especially nervous. He would pace back and forth, as was his wont. We were all worried about him, and we may have appeared to take Sylvia's imminent arrival as a matter of course. After all, she was number five!

When I was far away one time on a business trip to Mexico City, I missed the most dramatic incident of Sylvia's childhood. She was less than a year old and had accidentally turned on the hot water faucet as she was having her bath in the sink. Elaine heard the screams and rushed in to turn off the scalding water, no doubt castigating herself for having stepped out momentarily. Sylvia was severely burned and ended up in the hospital. They kept her in isolation for a week because the doctor felt that if she saw her mother she would want to come home with her. She might have carried this trauma with her through life, but she claims no physical or emotional scars.

Sylvia became fascinated with baking when she was three or four years old. She wanted to help her mom, whose baking was legendary in our family. This became a lifetime passion of hers; so many times I have enjoyed the fresh-baked aromas and tastes of the goodies from her oven.

I can't recall a single instance when Sylvia ever gave us a problem. She has told me that as a child she saw herself as being the "good girl" of the family. Some of this, she feels, was because so much attention was given to her sister Sigrid. Sylvia developed a wonderful talent for connecting with people in a positive way, which became the foundation for her careers of service to others. As a social worker, she was a counselor for battered women, directed a local unit of the Big Brother/Big Sister organization, and supervised social work for the State of Wisconsin's HIV/Aids Resource Center.

When Elaine was in her final years and I was constantly on duty as caregiver, even though a hired health aid came every day, Sylvia sensed we needed her. She took some time off and came from Wisconsin to help. She was like an angel sent by the Lord. Sylvia was a wonderful companion for Elaine (and for me) and continued to delight us with her baking, filling the house with tempting aromas. She helped with the shopping. She sang. She played Jotto and other word games with her mother. She was witness to the coming and goings of our corps of helpers, including our pastor who brought us the sacrament of communion.

While I connect with each of my offspring through music in different ways, to be sure, it may be that Sylvia's specialty of singing merges with my love of song. What fun for me to accompany her with an aria here and a pop song there. I have heard her break into a familiar hymn (or sometimes even a brand-new one) as she leads a discussion group and welcomes us all to join in—sometimes even to dancing in the aisle.

I was a proud and grateful dad to have her tell me that she was choosing the Lutheran ministry as a second career. Her husband Chris Lee-Thompson had preceded her in this calling, so she knew exactly what she was getting into. Following four years as a theological student at Wartburg Seminary, she was ordained in the summer of 2007 and can identify herself now as *Pastor Sylvia!*

As a pastor of a much earlier era, Sylvia's grandfather, the Rev. C. G. Naeseth, would have been aghast at the thought of women in the Lutheran ministry. How would he have reacted if he had known that his own granddaughter would one day succeed him as a spiritual leader of the same parish where he was pastor for thirty-five years? Amazingly, Sylvia was called to Spring Prairie Lutheran Church and she is now literally following in his footsteps. She and Chris are living in the same large parsonage where Sylvia's mother, Elaine, grew up. (Chris commutes daily to his parish, Hope Lutheran, less than a half hour away.) I believe C.G. would rejoice with us. Like us, he would surely melt with pride hearing her in the pulpit and seeing her officiate at the altar, communicating the Gospel with great sincerity, clarity, and positive presence. Mere coincidence or all a part of God's plan? Either way, all of us who knew and loved that gracious and spacious setting are thrilled. How I wish it had been during Elaine's lifetime.

I can identify with our number six child, Paul, who is the youngest of our brood, as I was the youngest of seven. The baby of the family is often advantaged and often disadvantaged. The last child is nurtured by a whole group of siblings as well as parents, but the last child is also not given the attention the older kids inevitably get. Naturally, I found his arrival not a unique experience, as Peg's was. But it was also true that when he was alone at home with just Elaine and me, we could take him along on trips. When I took Paul to Disney World on the threshold of his teens, it was a delight for me to ride through that mythical kingdom with my own son.

When Paul was still a preschooler, I was fascinated to observe that his hands were always busy. He loved creating things. He had the knack of making paper sculptures and constructing little toy-like objects out of scrap wood.

Since childhood, Paul has had a love affair with bikes. He rode everywhere, and his enchantment with this salutary sport led him to find jobs at bike shops. He was a quick learner and knew the two-wheelers inside and out. He and his neighborhood friend Dean took long rides on the north and south shores of Long Island. And then, while still in high school, they planned to take off one summer to ride across the country—all the way to the West Coast. We may have had some trepidation, but we decided we could trust them to accomplish this ambitious challenge safely. And they did. He later told me that it was critically important to him that his father and mother trusted him. A few years ago he shared with me his journal pages documenting that trip. The reality of the trip was more scary than I had ever imagined.

It's gratifying to me to know that Paul's wife Rita is a bike enthusiast also. They have several tandem bikes (among literally dozens of single-seaters) and love to go out together on the trails and into the woods on one of their bicycles "built for two."

A bicycle he built for one, for me, was a surprise on my seventieth birthday. He thought I was then old enough to enjoy cycling, I guess. I did for some years, finding it relaxing and good exercise, but kept out of traffic and stayed close to home. His gift was very moving to me as a generous filial gesture.

Paul also loved cars. When he was learning to drive, we went to the usual parking lot where we would do our circling and parking exercises. And then, early on, I simply got out of the car and said, "Okay, it's your turn. Take it around the lot." He did it as if he were a veteran. He still is expert at diagnosing automobile problems, and when I need a new car, I consult him first.

Paul is a graduate electronics engineer and creates miracles related to computer robotics and all sorts of gadgets from aircraft to satellites. He doesn't talk much about his work because a lot of it is classified. But his knowledge is also of use to his father, who needs help in connecting modern gadgets and home entertainment centers. Paul doesn't send letters nor e-mails: "Why should I sit in front of a computer at home when I'm working on one all day long?" Nor is he especially voluble in conversation (except when liberated by an extra glass of wine), not often wanting to just chat for its own sake. When he phones, I know it is because he has something to say or ask. I treasure the calls when they do occur.

I remember one really precious heart-to-heart talk with Paul. I recall I was at the kitchen table when he phoned, and it was clear something special was on his mind. Usually he gets right to the point. This time I sensed he was struggling with something difficult for him to talk about. I simply waited, and then he came out with it.

He had suffered through an emotional encounter with a young fellow he had been trying to mentor. Now this Joe needed a tool for some repair job and came over to ask to borrow it. They hadn't faced one another for months. It turned out that he had been released from a detox hospital just a few days before. For Paul this seemed to be the moment to share with him how troubled and disappointed he was with how this guy had mishandled his life, already being tragically ruined by drugs, alcohol, and irresponsible conduct.

Paul felt he had handled the confrontation well, but he was disappointed that he had not revealed how much raw anger he really had. We tossed back and forth the whole matter of how to know when we are doing the right thing. This gave me the opportunity to affirm my trust in him.

We got to talk about Elaine and her level of insecurity—it was shortly before she died. He had only positive things to say about how she handled her motherhood. As he went on about how wonderful she had been, I was almost in tears. I hoped he might find a way to express this to her, though I knew it would be difficult for him because he is not comfortable with sharing his emotions. In this intimate conversation, I felt he was affirming me, too.

I have been fortunate lately to have spent precious time with my six impressive offspring. But I wish I could see my grandchildren more often. Sigrid's daughter Nina lives in Paris. One time on an overnight stop-over en route to Italy, I had the joy of a delightful evening there with her and her boyfriend Vincent, who cooked us a splendid dinner. Peg's son Jason works nearby in Manhattan and spends some weekends helping me in Baldwin. Richard's Kirsten is also close by, a student here at Fordham. The others—Peg's Aaron,

Richard's Daniel, and Sylvia's Peter and Michael—I rarely see. Yes, I sometimes can join them where they are, and they may fly in and out of New York on business, but that's not really enough.

Once Peter traveled with me to Wisconsin after his arrival in New York from six months in Europe. He was a good companion, and we bonded in a special way during that trip as we changed off driving those many miles. I even have great-grandchildren! Aaron is married and has two daughters, Kirsten and Lauren, and a step-daughter, Ashleigh, whose mom is Jena, Aaron's second wife. I don't feel old enough to have great-grandchildren, but it's wonderful to visualize a veritable future colony of my descendants.

When we look back, there are many things that we wish we had done that we didn't do. Fathers have a common guilt about not being able to spend enough time with the family. Papa is pained still that he had to be gone so much, leaving the family to fend for itself. Today under such circumstances, we would be on the phone as if it were a private line across the ocean. In those days, making a transatlantic call before the age of direct dial was an infrequent luxury. And father had a responsibility to his professional calling. Of course, that was understood by all. But it didn't prevent my feeling that lonesome ache that came when I was away from home.

What might we have done differently? The sins of the parents have to be faced honestly in any such audit of parenting. I know that as part of our Lee family ethos, we recognize how essential forgiveness is. Even though each of us can claim some guilt—some may tend to claim more than they need to—forgiveness, I believe, has covered most of the hurts and wounds and resentments that may have arisen. We haven't had formal rituals of absolution (in our family, at least).

Knowing where and when to offer guidance was key to parenting for us. I hope we found an acceptable balance. I don't know if my sons and daughters agree, but I think I avoided excessive direction and control of them while they were growing up. While all small children need help along the way, growing up means acquiring decision-making skills. Fortunately, each of our progeny was intellectually gifted, and they mostly worked out their own procedures for navigating through both childhood and adolescence. None of them ever said, "The only reason I am doing this is because my daddy said I had to!" The record speaks for itself. I am personally proud of these capable, loving, and morally upright characters bred in our home.

Every now and then I have had the joy and fun of observing some trick or quirk or stylistic response that may actually have come from me. Some good, some bad, no doubt. And this octogenarian father can confess that he has modeled some of his ways from one or more of the Lee sextet. This emulation makes sense when I realize that the generation following Elaine's and mine is wiser and more knowledgeable and more competent than we ever were. Often—I am not kidding—I feel that they are the parent and I am the child.

Our children are a true gift from God to their mother and father.

L-R Paul, Sylvia, Richard Sigrid, Barbara, Peg, Bob

16 Celebration of Life

Normally I don't feel like celebrating life when I try to pry myself from my sleep and from my bed to begin my day. During the night I have two or three nature calls, but it is the clock that reminds me that my day is due to start. Whether I am or not!

Groggy with age and sleep, I might ask myself, "Is this the life?" But I don't ask that. Instead, my lazy conscience nudges me to sit up on the edge of the bed. Doing that reminds me that I have committed myself to make sitting there a spiritual moment as I arise, each new day.

So I make the sign of the cross (as Martin Luther suggests) and thank God for life. Yes, this *is* the life! And I have so much to thank God for: life itself, Elaine and our offspring and their spouses, my grandchildren, my great-grandchildren, my parents and siblings. I sneak in gratitude for my life and survival so far. I know it is a gift.

Then I literally stumble off for my morning toilette, stiff and aching and blurry. The routine happens as if on auto-pilot. Even though my sonic toothbrush beeps every thirty seconds (telling me it's time to choose the next quadrant of my dental display), I take off my watch so I can check the elapsed time, playing the game of guessing when the next beep will come. Once upon a time when I was a radio announcer I could "know" just when to wind up a thirty-second commercial pitch. These days, now that I have out-guessed the beeps, a clean mouth allows me to work my way to the kitchen to start the coffee-maker (unless I failed to set it up before sacking out last night).

I try to remember that it is important to do my exercises before I have breakfast. For years I have been dancing to Bach. Usually I choose the first allegro movement from a Brandenburg or violin or oboe concerto. But a couple of years ago I discovered in Italy, at Sigrid and Roberto's place, that one of their CDs was ideal for my exercises. It is, of all things, a Celtic folk song, "The Bonny Swans," sung by Loreena McKennitt. It is reassuring to me, as I dance past a full-length mirror on my bedroom door, to discover that, in spite of my moaning and groaning earlier, I am now actually smiling. It gives me hope for the day.

My exercising does not mimic gym-type workouts, but rather, as suggested by my doctor twenty years ago, dancing to the music. He really didn't prescribe "dancing" *per se*, but rather shadow-boxing to music. So when I tried that, it led by itself into moving around in a lively fashion. Now I dance all over the house with the music loud enough to be heard in every room (not when I have guests sleeping upstairs, of course, but I am alone almost all the time, so no one cares). I am now awake and can honestly tell myself this: "It's great to be alive!"

I used to be in denial about my age. Many told me I looked younger than I was. I resisted recognizing that I had become an octogenarian. I guess I feared ageism, the subtle feeling that old means feeble—the "old fogey" syndrome—in mind and body. I sensed that there was a small element of disparagement in how others saw us elderly folk. I resisted, almost resented, being put on the shelf.

I was wrong, of course. I had let my ego introduce an unsupportable phobia. The conversion for me came when I reached the age of eighty-five. I had the dawning of a new perspective on my seniority. I decided to celebrate my age, finally, rather that pretend I was younger that I really was. It may be a mistake, but now I find that I even volunteer letting people know I am eighty-five. I am discovering that, for many, that open awareness of my age evokes—among other things I might not choose to know—some respect, at the very least.

While Elaine was in her final years, coping with progressive strokes, I tried to send regular health bulletins on her situation to my family, mostly by e-mail. In the late 1990s when I was in my late seventies, I had just had a thorough annual physical exam by my doctor of over twenty years, the kind of physician who would schedule discussion groups at his Manhattan apartment and invite selected patients of his to join the group. I appreciated participating in a couple of those fascinating sessions kicking around current issues of politics, war, and peace. I decided to give my family a report on my own health:

> The short report is that everything is good, very good! My doctor said I had the health of a twenty-five-year-old. "I sure don't feel like it," I replied. He probed into the stresses in my life. When I explained Elaine's deterioration since her most recent stroke, he counseled me regarding my own psychological health. (His wife's own mother hasn't recognized her for five years, he said.) When I commented that I have always had a positive attitude and that right now I certainly need to employ it, he responded that he sensed the spiritual was important to me. I told him that Elaine and I get inspiration and help from the scriptures and hymns—I mentioned that she had been a church organist. And then, as if to echo his appreciation of

that element, he told me (after we had talked about the lab results), "You are an inspiration to me!" I replied, "Doctor, you are an inspiration to me, so we're even!"

Some of my earlier fixation on being younger than my contemporaries (I don't mean that as an oxymoron) comes from my November birthday. Because of that, I am always behind: most of my school classmates were a year older than I. So when I entered college, it was easy to pretend I was "grown up." It was only natural for me to fall in love with Elaine, who was already a sophomore when I was a freshman. Very few ever knew that she was three years older than her husband.

We children of Knute and Mathilda Lee have had a heritage of longevity. Mother lived ninety-five years, and, even though our father passed away early at age sixty, six of us seven have lived into our eighties and nineties. While both Margaret and Bill succumbed in their early eighties from Alzheimer's disease, three of my sisters survived longer, two of them still going strong today. Barbara, Juliet, and Naomi were known affectionately as the "Queens," a term of endearment coined by Naomi's late husband Niles. The sibling trio lived in separate homes in Rochester, Minnesota, near some of the best medical care in the world and only a few hours away from their childhood home.

I could not tempt them to visit me in New York. They may have shared the phobia of many Midwesterners for our wicked East Coast metropolitan regions—crime and traffic and noise and too many people! So I went to them. On every one of my frequent pilgrimages to visit them in Minnesota, I sensed the love of my sisters for their kid brother—notwithstanding my status as an octogenarian.

Naomi and I, the closest in age, first bonded as the two remaining Lee children at our Spring Grove home when our older brother and sisters were out working in the world or getting additional education. Naomi and Niles lived near us in Minneapolis, and a few years later in New York we were again neighbors. Being close to them was important to me because most of my family was in the Midwest. Niles was away a lot, as I was, so Naomi and Elaine faced a common problem of maintaining a family by themselves. Naomi and I had deep discussions about life, marriage, children, and even religion. Today Num and I still love to share ideas—eschewing trivia as far as possible. I am grateful for these intimate conversations, especially precious now that we are both without our spouses.

Sister Julie, deputy mother, at age eleven

Julie was my surrogate mother. She claims she raised me from infancy, showing me off in the village as she wheeled my baby carriage around. I have learned that whenever I visit Rochester Julie expects me to stay at her home. Her upstairs loft is "my" room, with the luxury of my own bathroom. I love the view of the city park, with strollers, runners, and bikers moving up and down the winding Bear Creek that bisects the city.

Julie's hospitality is legendary. She prepares for my visit (or anyone else's visit, no doubt) by having the table set and the coffee all ready. She will have a delicious lunch or supper table ready for steaming hotdishes from the oven. I can expect a Jello salad, with fine chopped fruits and nuts. And cookies. Always cookies. After every breakfast she always says, "I always finish breakfast with a cookie. Wouldn't you like one?" Who could resist the cookie jar she holds out, with its home-baked sweetness?

Within the first fifteen minutes after my arrival, she will say, "Well, you better sit down at the piano." Julie and I have in common our passion for music, especially piano improvising. She knows how I love to do just that. To me it means I have come home!

Sister Barbara lived ninety-seven years and impressed everyone who met her with her sharp intellect and—in certain circumstances—her sharp tongue. Of all those in our family, she was the most like our mother, Mathilda. We all were amazed when she insisted on hip replacement surgery at ninety-five. We had wondered if she could recover, but she was determined to risk it—the pain cried out for relief—and she won, enjoying life for several more years. She passed away in March 2006, just prior to her birthday.

Four remaining siblings. And then there were three

The trio of my siblings maintained a kind of symbiotic interdependence. Comfortably housed there in Rochester, they were able to give each other the support and reassurance of family. They would communicate daily in person or at least by phone. Julie, next door to Barbara, would check on her older sister each morning; mid-morning coffee was a standard ritual at one house or the other. Now it is Naomi who daily checks in with her older sister Juliet.

By their example the Queens have conveyed to me that life before and after reaching ninety can still be fulfilling and pleasurable. Each of the three was a widow, and I, their younger brother, a widower. Each sister was living alone, and so was I. Both Barbara and Juliet had remarried after their first husbands had died. And their second life-partners had succumbed also. They had the "Mathilda" fortitude that, along with their solid Christian faith, carried them through the double sorrow. Naomi's husband, Niles, died from cancer several years ago. Mourning their spouses with dignity and moving into the healing aftermath, they have been powerful models for me.

We elderly folk seek comfort and security as priority needs. They had it, and it helped me appreciate that I have it also. We are fortunate to have solicitous and caring family members who grace our lives by their visits—always attending to fixing things in our homes or accomplishing tasks that are daunting for us seniors. Our homes are filled with good memories—both tangible mementos and abundant memories covering most of the last century. God is blessing our sunset years.

My oldest sister, Sylvia, didn't live long enough to experience sunset years. She died at age fifty-six in 1964. On June 10, 2007, we marked the hundredth anniversary of her life. Her finale was laced with painful cancer. I remember wanting so much to see her one last time before she died; on a business trip to Minnesota, I detoured to my home county. She had been working in Caledonia, our county seat, but she and her husband Fremont Deters lived on their farm in the nearby hamlet of Eitzen. I spotted her in the village as she was getting into her car. I thought she would recognize me, but she didn't, apparently, or chose not to.

When after a decent interval, I drove out to their farm—it was raining heavily that spring day—I encountered a problem: I was unable to drive up the muddy road to their house. A farm truck had to come and take me up to the house. It was strange being there. She didn't seem glad to see me. She was somehow aloof, not at all like the Sylvia I knew, and she repaired to a couch. Clearly she was in pain, and I realized that the pain was behind her distancing herself from me. I didn't linger long. She must have felt embarrassed and wanted her kid brother to remember her as before.

One of my fondest memories of Sylvia was from 1955, when she came out to our home in Baldwin at the time our own daughter Sylvia was born. She was there—I think at my invitation—to help Elaine and our family with our fifth child. She remained through the baptism; appropriately, Sylvia was her namesake's sponsor at the ceremony.

I am saddened that neither sister Margaret nor brother Bill could enjoy these enriching years of survival. Alzheimer's robbed both of them of communicative joy and social connections with family, friends, and the lively contemporary world. Yet I am grateful that they received tender comforting care from their family and from the staffs of their respective nursing homes. There is some solace for me in my having visited them there. I wasn't ever certain if they knew I was Bob, their brother. Bill in his wheelchair seemed vacant, heavy in weight and spirit, rarely allowing a smile. Margaret in her wheelchair seemed always to wear a smile. While neither could carry on a conversation with me, our eye contact somehow allowed us to exchange the spiritual force of love.

With both Margaret and Bill, I found that singing seemed to connect best emotionally. A softness came to their eyes when melody was heard and rhythm was felt. Human touch also elicited a response. Their spouses, Paul and Shirley, were constant in spending time with their often unresponsive loved ones, helping to feed them at mealtimes. Each had wanted to care for their life-mate at home, but they came to the point where it was beyond their capability, so a nursing home was the only logical alternative. Fortunately, the institution in both cases was staffed by gentle, understanding aides, usually chattering away in cheery, upbeat voices as they ministered to patients.

Naturally, I couldn't help imagining myself in such a situation. I pray it won't happen, both for my sake and for the sake of my family. Although the patients perhaps reach a point of oblivion to their condition, who knows what dreams still live in their souls? God only knows what each person's finale will be.

In 1990 I thought the end of my life might be imminent. I was diagnosed with prostate cancer. This, of course, was a blow to me personally and also to Elaine. We accepted this frightening news with equanimity, at least on the surface. We were living in an age where medical science offers miracles of healing. After the usual round of tests and internal exploration, I was told that surgery to remove the cancerous prostate would be my best way of survival. After much prayer and discussion, and depending on my faith, I submitted to the doctors' higher wisdom.

I tried to be strong and brave about this whole procedure, but I had overestimated my bravado. I needed to be alone. I have a precious memory of taking a long, prayerful walk the day before I went into the hospital. I sat down in the park in the shade of an inviting tree. And that was where I cleansed my soul with tears. It helped.

Undergoing this process was a first time in the hospital for me. I was curious, but I was also apprehensive—it was a profound reminder of my mortality. It never hurts to consider mortality thoughtfully and prayerfully as the limits of God's gift of life. I worried more about Elaine's reaction because I recognized her emotional vulnerability. I was proud and gratified at my family's evidence of support. All in all, the surgery experience and its aftermath were remarkable as events of consequence in my life.

One important consequence for Elaine and me was the change in our sexual life. This was 1990, and loss of potency could be expected following a prostatectomy. But we came to recognize that two lovers could still find ways to share themselves with each other. We learned that the physical and psychic treasures within a loving sexual compact are God's gift worthy of thanksgiving.

Half way through the next fifteen years, the reality changed for me again when I learned that cancer had broken through its earlier remission state and needed attention. My urologist who had performed the prostate surgery on me eight years previously was retiring, and I had my final session with him. I was troubled and very disappointed to learn that my PSA (Prostate Specific Antigen) had shot up to four from one plus. What did this mean? Was my cancer returning? Clearly there were some cancer cells loose in my body. I had expected the excision of the malignant source to have completely eliminated the dread disease. I said nothing about it at home and put it behind me for further consideration later.

The following year I had another session with my urologist, who warned of my rising index of the PSA. Some rogue cells, supposedly dormant following my surgery almost a decade earlier, were now actually metastasizing somewhere in my body. I needed a second opinion to help choose among therapy options—one of which was to do nothing. My primary doctor referred me to an oncologist who proved wonderfully helpful and positive about the whole thing. We would work out a plan. For the time being, I opted not to mention this to any of the family. They didn't need this extra concern on top of Elaine's perilous condition.

I was somewhat relieved to have my cancer situation clarified. I didn't want to worry about it, feeling that I must not ignore taking action if there was action to take. I felt I was in good hands. In good hands, indeed....

The oncologist came in the examining room and probed and listened and touched and did what I think is called a full-body review or something like that. He was feeling for abnormalities all over the body, and he pounded and touched and felt with what I assume are his trained and educated fingers. Then we went back in his office to talk.

The overall conclusion is that right now I should wait and, given my personal situation, not go for radiation. If the cancer cells are in the prostate "bag," then directing radiation at them could get rid of them all. But how would we know they have not gone elsewhere in the body? Right now there are no symptoms apparent to indicate this. My PSA is still within the tolerance limit ... and radiation has side effects, and we talked about those.... His general advice seems to be to watch it, continue as I am with regular sessions with him and get in touch with him if circumstances change and symptoms appear.

He pointed to my family heritage of longevity—my mother's long life and my sisters', etc. He felt this was important. I can now, I think, be at peace because I know I am doing everything I can about this that is reasonable. Worry and fretting will not help but could hinder extending life. I am accepting a circumstance I cannot change. I guess that means that there is room for faith. And I thank God for the gift of faith.

For the last ten years this wonderful doctor has continued to walk me through careful control of the marauding cancer cells so that life is reasonably normal.

The renewed cancer was one of my life's pivotal events. In my case this emotional and physical setback has proved to be an initiative for growth. I believe that I have grown in understanding myself, am better able to examine my life, and am drawn closer to my God. I sense that I have gained a fresh and rejuvenated spirituality. It seeps into my prayers, enriches my participation in church, and colors my basic attitude toward life.

On the wall of my living room I live daily with a painting done by the late Ben Shahn, one of America's great social artists of the twentieth century. When I needed a decorative setting for a Lutheran theme to observe the 450th anniversary of the Reformation, he painted for me this piece of art that fits his style of using English or Hebrew lettering in his work, here in his distinctive and colorful floral-folk setting: LIFE—NEW LIFE!

Each day when I look at this, I sense that I am enjoying my new life more, not only in these sunset years, but also in each new day of grace. It is God's precious gift to me.

I have adopted another set of words to use as a spiritual reminder each day of this "new" life. These words sum up for me the mystery and miracle of faith given to us. While I try to express my gratitude to God each morning, I find that it lingers best in my mind with these words:

An attitude of gratitude.

17 Sunset Reflections

I live alone. I like the house that I've lived in for over half a century. It meets my needs. I have a cozy office with all the equipment I need, a basement that is full of junk that some day will have to be cleared out, a convenient first floor bedroom, and room upstairs for family and guests. Most first-time visitors comment favorably on my sunroom, which is a restful place to sit when it's not too cold in the winter or too hot in the summer. When I have forty or fifty people together here, they can find a number of conversation areas for a semi-private chat, especially in the summertime when we expand to the back lawn and the patio.

Many people have asked me when I am going to move to a smaller place, but I am comfortable here. I find the kitchen in the morning wonderfully enticing when it's flooded with sunshine. I cook the simplest of meals. As a coffee addict, I make sure the beverage is always available. In order not to overdo my enjoyment of the brew, I never take more than a half cup at a time, but that means I take many half cups! Because I live alone, I sometimes don't have my shower and dress until noon. I find it very comforting to sit down at the piano and play either hymns or pop songs from yesteryear, or doodle on an improvisation. And during the day I can take naps in a recliner in the living room with beautiful stereo music serenading me. Sometimes I wake up and discover that it's dusk, and through my picture windows I see a glorious sunset.

For over fifteen years, I had my office upstairs in the largest of four bedrooms. I had it set up with TV-VCR-stereo, computer, scanner, phones, copy machine, and, before they became unneeded, a fax machine. I had books and tapes up there, two working desks, and too many filing cabinets jammed with a lifetime of accumulated papers. I have discovered that going up and down stairs is more onerous than it was a few years ago. So I have moved my office downstairs. Almost every piece of equipment I need is now down here.

This residence, like most family homes, is rich in memorabilia. As I look around my rooms, there are constant reminders of Elaine—sheet music on the piano, dictionaries and reference books on the shelves, cooking utensils in the kitchen. Large blowup photos on my office wall hold her in my active memory.

Of course I couldn't ever forget, even without pictures. But I am no longer in mourning. I have healed. I am looking ahead, planning writing projects, and trying to schedule some travel. I have an active e-mail correspondence and even some by post.

I can't complain. Well, I confess to little complaints like my aches and pains and the possibility that my cancer may grow. Meanwhile spinal stenosis, with annoying back and leg aches, keeps me humble (or reasonably humble).

Once upon a memory...
songs & hymns from Elaine and Bob Lee

In Memoriam
ELAINE 1919-2000

REAL WORLD COMMUNICATIONS

Back when my voice was in full force and Elaine's voice and piano were as smooth and subtle as they could be, she and I recorded some songs to send to my mother. Sigrid made those ancient audio tapes into a CD. A memorial to Elaine, it carried the title *Once Upon a Memory*. The first song on that CD, a duet with the two of us backed by her piano accompaniment, has an ironic application for me now. Six years after her death I hear this very sentimental recording with her voice and mine singing these words from the nineteenth century American ballad, "In the Gloaming":

> In the gloaming, oh, my darling, when the lights are dim and low
> And the quiet shadows falling softly come and softly go.
> When the winds are sobbing faintly with a gentle, unknown woe,
> Will you think of me and love me as you did once long ago?
>
> In the gloaming, oh, my darling, think not bitterly of me.
> 'Though I passed away in silence, left you lonely, set you free.
> For my heart was thrust in longing—what had been, could never be.
> It was best to leave you thus, dear. Best for you and best for me.
>
> It was best to leave you thus ... best for you and best for me.

Romantic music aside, I am not ready to concede that it was "best for me." But as the survivor, I try to live each day by faith. I resonate to the old German chorale (and Bach cantata) *Gottes Zeit is die allerbeste Zeit* (God's time is the very best time). I accept that her death was merciful, knowing that Elaine was saved more suffering from her illness. As we sang together, "It was best to leave you thus...."

Shortly before Elaine died we joined St. Peter's Lutheran Church, just a few blocks up the street. The people there have embraced me (many of them quite literally), and good friendships have developed. I was enticed to join the choir. I thought my singing days were over, but I found that I could still sing reasonably well. I found much pleasure in rehearsing music together with the dozen or so who sing anthems from the back balcony. We have been blessed with excellent cantors (organist and choir leaders), and our organ is a bona fide pipe organ and not what Elaine sometimes described derisively as "an electronic appliance."

And our Pastor Ed Barnett, young and single, is more than my spiritual leader. He is a good friend. He enjoys studying ecclesiology—the nature of the organized church. He thinks I know everything about how the churches are organized. Though I never found bureaucracy attractive, I made my peace with it and discovered I could work the system as well as the next person. Well, I have been away from that scene for almost twenty years now in my retirement, so my information is moldy. But I understand Ed's special interest in church politics. I always enjoy our conversations, rare because they have depth. Pastor Ed has added a bright dimension to these years for me.

Before Elaine died, our family met with an attorney, an elder-law specialist. He advised us on the realities in light of Elaine's illness. After Elaine's passing, I remember his asking me, "What are some of the things you really want to do?"

He was referring to the fact that I was now relatively free to pursue some of my dreams, at least to the extent that my savings would allow. I immediately answered, "I would like to be able to travel and visit with my family near and far." So I have done that and hope to continue modestly. Since I became a widower, I have visited Europe twice and have gone to see friends and relatives in Florida, Texas, California, Nevada, the Midwest, and New England. I have just returned from a visit with Sigrid and Roberto in Italy.

I enjoy a limited social life and have gone to concerts, seen movies, and have accepted party invitations. I have inaugurated an annual Summer Solstice Party each June for about sixty friends.

I have been surprised at some of the directions that my retirement has taken me. For example, I'm a late bloomer in eclectic art appreciation. Maybe this is what retirement is supposed to be about—catching up with soul delights previously lost in the shuffle of earning daily bread.

It's not that I now spend my non-productive hours basking in unread classics or building a CD library of new sounds or touring galleries touting postmodern canvases. Nothing that intentional. Rather, my new discoveries have unobtrusively insinuated themselves into days already brimming over with fascinations and the maintenance demands of latter-day singlehood.

Just today I paused to take stock. What's different?

I have been listening to some wonderful jazz on the radio. While that musical genre has always been of some passing interest (the take-it-or-leave it type), suddenly I seem mesmerized by the nuances of Wynton Marsalis' elegant interpretation of "Guess I'll Hang My Tears out to Dry" and a whole series of bouncing, buttery ballads dressed up in syncopated jazz. Knowing that some of the top classical artists like Marsalis, Yo Yo Ma, and even conductors like Andre Previn can be equally brilliant when playing jazz has helped me elevate in my own scale of values this creative category to the high art status it deserves.

I have roamed through art galleries off and on all my life, here and abroad, but only recently have I really studied some of the spectacular art hanging in New York galleries and museums. It is exciting finally to apprehend Jackson Pollack and to realize his art is more than random splashes of paint.

Where have I been all my life and not read the poetry of Czeslaw Milosz, whom I discovered only when I read he had died? And hearing the former Poet Laureate Ted Kooser from Nebraska being interviewed on the Jim Lehrer News Hour on PBS, I was stimulated by his talking about reading and writing poetry. His words got me going, and I think I have now been captured by a new passion.

A news item drew me to the Brooklyn Academy of Music, where I was enthralled by a new musical setting of the biblical passion story for soloists, chorus, orchestra, and even dancers. It was the premiere in this area of Argentinean composer Osvaldo Golijov's highly dramatic "Passion of St. Mark." Hearing this contemporary work, commissioned by the Stuttgart Bach maestro Helmut Rilling, with its wild Latin rhythms and emotional valleys and dramatic peaks, was an inspiring revelation. Only after the work was over and the composer was called on stage by the long applauding listeners did I realize that all during the concert he was sitting right in front of me.

I have seen hundreds of exquisite and profound photographs over the course of many years, but only recently have I come to prize this art medium as very "fine art" indeed. Black-and-white film seems more classic somehow, especially on gallery walls or in folio collections or coffee table books. But two of my daughters, who have been exhibiting startling color images taken with their digital cameras, have gifted me with many chromatic moments of awe, now unfolding daily on my computer as screen-saver art.

While there was a time when I saw most new movies to come along, now I miss most of the good ones. But when a film buff friend of mine eagerly relates the story of the latest picture he just saw and insists to me that it is a "must see," I try to go. The idea of cinema as recreation rather than professional responsibility is refreshing. And that's how I discovered one of the finest productions to brighten the screen in years—an offbeat British movie, "Vera Drake," which wrapped me in its emotional realism and left me weak from wrestling with vicarious human drama. Yes, you "must see" it—but I fear that, like so many fine films, it may not survive without blockbuster hype to promote it.

Even modern dance has dazzled me in a new way. Watching the stunning choreography of Paul Taylor or Mark Morris being danced at Lincoln Center has made me wish I had been a subscriber years ago.

And opera, which it seems I had just tolerated before, has suddenly opened for me a new musical-theatrical experience: a world in which the incredible accomplishments of lyricists and composers are sensitively synthesized with dramatic and love-lifting vocalists, using the top talents of instrumentalists and conductors, choruses, stage directors, costumers, and set designers. Why had I sometimes discounted opera as "screaming sopranos"?

Please don't think that I am just a neophyte aficionado of music, painting, sculpture, architecture, literature, dance, poetry, photography, or even cinema. Cultural appreciation has always been important. But when the pace of a busy life shoved so much of artistic value to the side in favor of producing work results, culture could not be front and center except when it appeared on my job description—as it did when I reviewed at least one movie each week for several years in the 1970s and 1980s. Now that the daily commuting grind is behind me, I find gifts of new art waiting to surprise me down the street and just around the next corner.

I plan to continue to make the most of it.

"In My Solitude" at the beach

In facing the basic question of what I really want to do with my life at this point, I have rediscovered that I love to write. Writing gives me a stimulus I can't get any other way. Since completing *Mathilda's Journey*, the story of my mother that was published in the year Elaine died, I have written and had published *Dear Elaine* and am now on the final chapter of this fourth draft of *My Wings at Sunset*. Barbara is my editor. She goes over every page and every word with me. I welcome our collaboration to make my text more interesting and readable. When she agreed to be my editor, I fear she didn't know what she was getting into. Stand by, dear, I have several book ideas I intend to tackle next, God willing!

My kids told me that when they were small and impressionable they used to love the New Year's Eve story I revived on the last night of each year. The first protagonist was the Old Man/Old Year with a long white beard and scythe. Just what did that represent—mowing down all the old weeds and dead grass from the months past? Only later did I learn that the Old Man was the medieval figure representing Death.

I had fun acting out the roles in the New Year's story. I limped out of the room as the Old Man going "over the hill." And then I reappeared in new guise as the Baby/New Year. I think we celebrated with applause and laughter and shouts and songs. Later I was asked to recreate the story for two of my grandsons. I'm not sure it had the same creative energy, although the Old Man role may have been more convincing than before.

How to look at this annual ritual of passage at midnight of December 31? A time for reflection, evaluation, resolution … Musings, if we take the time for them, can be cathartic, therapeutic, and even hopeful. Or, depending upon our situation, wearying, woeful, or even tearful.

Life is usually represented as a journey, traveling toward something. I find that the closer we get to the top of the hill, the less eagerly we approach the summit. We want to look back. I fear we bore younger ears with our recitation of what we see in the rear-view mirror. But in our daily viewing of television, we can't escape the replay of two world wars and other military conflicts that shook the planet. As we see the dreadful carnage continuing in each day's headlines, the conclusion has to be that there is a lesson in the past that has to be relearned. All of us in every generation need to weigh the implications of the past. *Turn Back, O Man* …

And while we don't always focus on that point ahead, we know that it is the terminal of the journey. Life's journey is not a simple trip, but is crowded with diversions along the way. I like the concept shared with me by a friend: our life not seen as straight-line linear but, rather, as non-linear—a kind of total Internet-like experience, a collection of meaningful moments.

I once heard the German "theologian of hope" Jurgen Moltmann invite us to visualize the future not as our going to meet it but rather as it coming to meet us. Advent, you know, and all that. I find that sort of imaging difficult. The future is so terribly abstract. Who can describe it?

Life—New Life. Lots to think about in those three little words. *Life*—the old year and years stretching way back (at least for me) and then *New Life*—the future ahead. The newness is loaded with possibility, opportunity, a new beginning, and even an ending with heavenly visions! I hear the echo of my family singing the table prayer, "For life and health and every good we give you thanks, O Lord." If I can carry that over the hill with me, it's probably enough.

I am often reminded, because I am in my mid-eighties, that my expected span of life may already have expired. But I haven't expired, and I pray I can live for more years. I love life. But I try to be a realist. As a cancer survivor, I often feel I am already living on "borrowed time." Each of us is, to a certain extent. I would be a fool if I didn't face the possibility that I could meet my Thanatopsis moment any day.

I have talked about this with my children. I have begun a file into which I tuck notes of some of my life-closure thoughts as they come to me. My daughters Peg and Barbara will be the administrators of my estate. Meanwhile, Barbara advises me on financial matters and sets me straight with my bank accounts and checkbook. What a gift that is for me, as I never was very good at math and financial records. Now that she has retired, she has more time to fuss helpfully with her father's business. We talk on the phone almost every day.

I try not to think of some of the possibilities I may meet. I could suffer a lingering, painful illness. I could be incapacitated, so I would need help in walking, talking, and eating. I know what is involved in that and hope I can escape it. But we don't have options of our own to choose among. Life itself is a gift given to us by God and the decisions must be his. I try to help by maintaining a reasonable life style, by regular checkups and physicals. I have monthly sessions and shots from my oncologist. I have a neurologist, who, at my most recent session, told me: "You're in good shape. Live a good life. Enjoy good wine!" I laughed. He smiled.

This is the sunset time of my life. I still see the glorious coloration of the sky out there in the Pacific over sixty years ago. And I can still sing: "My Wings at Sunset ... will carry me home!"

An old Norwegian folk hymn has fitting words for this sunset or gloaming time of day and time of life. The music and words, memorized long years ago and sung often with Elaine, come back hauntingly now:

> The sun has gone down
> And peace has descended on country and town;
> The songbirds in silence have flown to their nest
> And flowers are closing their petals in rest;
> So closes my heart to annoyance and care,
> In homage and prayer, in homage and prayer.
>
> I praise for this day
> The Father in heaven, who prospered my way,
> Who shielded from danger, protected from harm,
> Promoted my labor, and strengthened my arm;
> For hours that passed lightly as birds on the wing,
> Thanksgiving I bring, thanksgiving I bring.

APPENDIX
Bob's Gallery of Mentors

Preparing a memoir offers the writer a rare opportunity to examine his life. In the process, he realizes the influence that others have had on him—parents, spouse, children, grandchildren, siblings, pastors, teachers, friends, colleagues and myriad others who have entered his life space. For me, my mentors over the years loom large in the lasting effect they had on my growth, training, and values. Personalities parade through my consciousness as I summon back their faces, voices, and the lingering lessons they taught me. I cannot possibly in fairness name them all. I have chosen to single out a few for whom I feel a special gratitude. Most can no longer hear my "Thanks!"

Oscar Mikkelson

Mikky came into my life about the time I was age ten as my teacher, pastor, scoutmaster, and friend. I went to his class with most others in my grade out to a small building near the school, where religion could be taught as long as it was not the State of Minnesota doing it. They called it released-time. In his low-key, cozy way, Pastor Mikky lathered us youngsters with a fresh spirituality as he shared his wisdom and gave us his take on the mysteries of Scripture. Later, as our pastor, he modeled for me an enviable posture of strength and manhood with lively intellectual curiosity. He went to war, too, and was a chaplain in Europe. I treasure a long letter he wrote from there to me out in the Pacific.

> From your letter it's obvious that your life is filled with excitement. It's such a "strange interlude" in a person's life, isn't it? To think of you soaring in the clouds looking for action is entirely out of tune. It's different with Bill because of the differences in your temperaments. You always leaned toward the quieter, the more aesthetic. Might I say in complement, the "Jacob" side, and yet life has brought

you face to face with what demands so much of a man physically as well as mentally. It's to your credit that you can meet it all with such excellent fortitude.

Some day, if God wills it, we shall gather again in that parsonage and shoot the breeze. I'd give what pounds I have in my pocket right now just to hear Bill laugh. We'd best plan a reunion, the Lees and the Mikkelsons. It was almost the same family, you know. Guess it was our affinity of minds that made us so much at home with one another. Let's not allow this vile intrusion into the quietude of our home lives to change us to the extent that we no longer can lie on the floor, or with our feet over the chairs, and laugh heartily at the pure nonsense of a good story.

Once the war was over, life changed radically for each of us. I was married and was busy as a radio announcer, Bill was a student again and aimed at becoming a minister like Mikky, who soon moved on to another pastorate. So, alas, we never did accomplish those moments of delicious relaxation together.

Paul Heltne

Paul was tall, slender, and handsome in his own way. With his high cheekbones and sparkling eyes, he had a charisma and charm that invited admiration from a twelve- or thirteen-year-old student. Now, in retrospect, I see his face—like a youthful-but-taller Frank Sinatra reflecting a certain vulnerability and tenderness. He was not the strong athletic type. Yet he could be jolly and flamboyant and displayed a lively sense of show business.

As my band director, he gave me a taste of music as a language for expressing the songs in my heart. I don't know how and when it happened, but we seemed to bond in what I felt was a relationship of respect unlike any I had previously experienced.

He was already my hero when I was in seventh or eighth grade, tutoring me as a budding trumpeter—though he himself played reeds rather than brass—and seemed to uncover my soul for music (My brother Bill had already taught me the elements of trumpet playing). I was inducted into the high school band before my time. I remember the thrill I had when he would give me the baton and let me direct a march, first in a rehearsal and once at a local concert. That told me that he trusted me.

He let me be his music librarian. A learning experience was that, to be sure. Outside of our band sessions, we discussed the marvelous world of music. He helped me gain a vision of music as a life accompaniment that could give me emotional sustenance and offer joy to others.

On the night of his death, March 19, 1985, Paul had given a speech on Christian witnessing to a church group in Austin. There were almost a thousand persons in the audience. His daughter found the notes for that speech that included these words:

> We witness in our work, our play, our human relationships, our business and social contacts; we witness every day by the examples we set in our speech and actions. We are all witnesses living in Christ.

Gudrun Muller

A local woman who returned to her hometown to teach, Miss Muller shared her love of learning with us youngsters who were at one of the most impressionable stages of life, junior high school. Gudrun was tall and, with her lively spirit, communicated that she was in charge. She was well known in our town and had been a star basketball player in high school. Muller's upbeat spirit infused itself into our character development. She sparkled with wit and scolded with an abrasive tongue. But mostly she revealed the values in her heart and allowed us to consider them for residence in our hearts as well.

I think of Gudrun Muller so often now when I hear a voice speaking in one of the familiar crisp and lilting Midwestern accents. The sound seems to be mimicking her own very Norwegian-flavored brogue. But it was she who warned us students against carrying the Minnesota accent into life and gave us antidotal vocal exercises—which she herself could have used! Those tips helped me immeasurably when I became a radio announcer.

Years later, after the war, while working for ELC Films in Minneapolis, I did some filming of her in Chicago where she was running a pre-school day-care center for disadvantaged children. It was a joy to follow her around with our 16 mm film crew to capture moments of her admirable work to include in a Lutheran social services educational movie. I was happy to see she had lost none of the witty and sharp-tongued teaching technique that I once feared, but loved as well, in junior high school.

I found a letter Gudrun had written that was published in the *Spring Grove Herald*. She congratulated me on the PBS network broadcast of my film, *The Joy of Bach*. She wrote about me as not only her former student but as "hometown boy makes good." It's a tribute I treasure.

Frank Gamelin

He was Professor Francis Gamelin when I first knew him as a speech teacher at Luther College, and he became the faculty supervisor of KWLC, the college radio station where I worked almost every day for my four undergraduate years. His was a warm, smooth, but animated mien that matched his expressive face. He was a splendid speech teacher dramatic coach, and I eagerly soaked up his exciting suggestions for my own vocal performances. He became a friend even then.

He took a group of us in our radio gang to the funeral of a classmate friend of ours who had died suddenly one night in our dormitory. He was the one in the college office who received the critical phone call from Spring Grove about my father's death in 1939. I wasn't on campus at the time, and Prof. Gamelin drove the streets of Decorah to find me. When he did, he gave me the news. I remember the warmth of his compassion.

Years later we renewed our friendship when both of us were church executives in New York City. We still correspond by letter and e-mail. I feel bonded with him in mutual admiration. In his most recent letter he wrote:

> We remain thankful, as we read your insightful writing, that we became acquainted with you early enough at Luther to follow your entire stellar career. Thanks for your friendship.

Carlo A. Sperati

I can still hear him in his guttural, Norwegian-flavored voice loudly proclaiming to us at rehearsals, "A place for everything and everything in its place!" Usually that was his rebuke when someone had misplaced some piece of music.

He was our Maestro in college, the dynamic old man whose baton called forth marvelous music from the concert band. He came with a story-book background: a Norwegian sailor whose mother was Norse and whose father was an Italian violinist at the Opera in Christiania (now Oslo). He had roamed the world on the high seas, and one time while in San Francisco in the late 1800s, he felt the call to the Lutheran ministry. That ultimately brought him to Luther College after his ordination, and he became a teacher and music director. His career was legendary.

Playing trumpet under the baton of Sperati was an invigorating experience for this small town boy. The Maestro was, for me, a model of musical leadership. I felt honored by his recognizing my potential in music. I was able to absorb many little nuances of performance and instrumental dynamics that accompanied me all my life.

I was very touched that Luther College sent Dr. Sperati as its representative to speak at my father's funeral. He made mention of my father's two sons, both of whom played in his band. Both Bill and I were honored by his words.

A vivid memory for me is his gathering a brass choir from his band, including this trumpeter, to climb to the top of the Winneshiek County Courthouse to play hymns to the city on Easter morning.

J. C. K. Preus

I still see him as a kind of modern biblical patriarch, the epitome of a leader with a confident bearing and a voice filled with resonant overtones. That voice could be strong both in prophetic proclamation and also in gentle encouragement. Johann Carl Keyser Preus was always Uncle Kalla to us. His wife Dikka (short for Diderikke) was the sister of Elaine's mother.

While I was broadcasting over WMIN in my first post-war job, we lived in St. Paul and often went over to Minneapolis to visit Aunt Dikka and Uncle Kalla. He had the Preus family natural charm—his three brothers were a former governor of Minnesota, the President of Luther College, and a seminary professor. Although I had known him even when I was in college, it was in the Twin Cities where I really felt his fatherly understanding of me. He was director of Christian Education of our Lutheran Church body. On one of our visits in 1947, he offered me a job I couldn't refuse: producing radio shows of dramatized Bible stories for children. It rescued me from the woes of commercial broadcasting, helped me find a professional home within my spiritual home, included Elaine's musical talent as a creative collaborator, and gave us a year in Montana.

When I was called back to Minneapolis, I was given an office next to his at the church headquarters. From that setting I not only was able to get his frequent counsel on theological questions, but had the opportunity to spend time with him in his office, at lunch, and at meetings. This allowed me to study his leadership technique. He was a kind, wise, and empathetic mentor, a guide who offered always affirmative advice and counsel.

Paul Empie

Paul Empie was one of the most influential leaders of American Lutheranism. He was head of the National Lutheran Council, and under that umbrella there was a whole group of independent sub-units. One of these was Lutheran Film Associates.

Coming to the East, I was the executive chosen by the LFA Board, of which Paul Empie was president. That meant I reported more or less to him as the embodiment of the Board. He gave me support and encouragement from the very beginning. Whenever I had some questions as to how to proceed or how to resolve a political dilemma, I would call him and inevitably feel reassured and helped. (Yes, there are lots of politics in church organizations, as in most other aspects of life.) Paul was solid in his analyses, clear in his explanations, and sincere in reaching out in friendship.

Paul traveled the world in connection with his work. I remember being in Berlin in 1954, less than a decade after World War II, when he flew in from Yugoslavia to visit at the same place where I was staying with our American contact. He brought us bottles of slivovitz, described by one writer as "exactly like butane with a licorice aftertaste!" I survived the taste test.

I also remember seeing a photograph somebody caught of Paul in Finland emerging from a cold water swim after a sauna. Over there, the uniform of the day in the sauna is no clothes at all! I remembered that later on when I was invited to a sauna club in Helsinki.

Empie stands in my estimation as a great churchman, a leader, a colleague, and a true friend. Each Christmas I received a note from him with a greeting, not commenting on my performance—he found other appropriate opportunities for doing that—but rather thanking me for my friendship. Without knowing he was doing it, I am sure, he taught me so much that helped me maneuver through the bureaucratic and ecclesiastical jungles where I labored. I am remembering his warm smile as he indicated the solution to a problem, as if to say, *This is how it's done!*

Henriette Lund

At our Lutheran Center in Manhattan everyone quickly knew that Henriette had arrived. I could hear her down the hall as she chatted with the staff at their desks, and soon this wizened woman in her nineties—always with her hat on—peeked into my space and came in to chat. I loved it. We found a lot in common. She had worked with Elaine's sister Margaret and her husband, who had been missionaries in Alaska. She always brought me a little token from one of her trips, like a smooth stone from an arctic beach as a paper weight for my desk.

She had been a pioneer in post-World War II resettlement of refugees. She had been a social worker among the poor in urban areas and among the downtrodden Eskimos in Alaska. She traveled the world and wrote articles and books. She championed the death of Apartheid within South Africa. She had picketed their United Nations Embassy in Manhattan. She worked in Geneva for the Lutheran World Federation and came to represent that organization in the non-governmental pool at the U.N. in New York.

She came to Baldwin to spend weekends with us. She gave our son Paul a real polar bear foot that he had fun with for years. She invited Elaine and me to her apartment on Water Street near the tip of Manhattan Island. She showed us the egg shells she saved, demonstrating how she would take the remains of egg white and with her fingers pat the gooey liquid on her face. "It keeps me young," she told us.

After her so-called retirement, Henriette kept going. She put in over seventy years of social service. She continued to travel and made six extensive visits to Eskimos in Alaska including one at age seventy-eight by dogsled and another at age ninety-one that resulted in two books. This is how she is quoted as describing retirement:

> You don't retire from something when you quit your work; you retire into something. You don't stop your work; you stop one phase of it for another.

When Henriette was near death, Elaine and I went to see her in the hospital and found her unconscious with only a breathing machine apparently keeping her alive. This upset us, and we talked it over with two of her close friends, both Lutheran pastors. I understand they talked to her doctors and convinced them that Henriette would not want to spend her last earthly days in a vegetative state. She mercifully passed away soon after.

F. Borden Mace

Borden Mace's soft and mellow North Carolina drawl was pleasant and distinctive to my Midwestern ears. I was impressed by the fact that this first Southerner I really came to know well was more advanced in his racial attitudes in the mid-1950s than most of us Northerners. He was the one who pointed out for me the significance of the Emmett Till case at the time. He proved to be prophetic.

As a new executive in New York I met with Borden on an almost daily basis. He was the president of Louise deRochemont Associates, well known film producers. My first office was down the hall from his on Madison Avenue in Manhattan. I found him a very creative leader. As a businessman with CPA credentials, he was a commercial realist. As a producer he was a sensitive, creative artist. He immersed himself in both entertainment and educational films. He was a perfect example of one who thinks outside the box. He set a pace for me that sometimes left me almost breathless. Borden and I stayed close. Each time we connect it seems that we are continuing an earlier conversation we had never finished. My friend Borden was kind, wise, understanding, helpful, supportive—all the things a mentor could and should be.

Lothar Wolff

When Lothar appears on my memory screen, we are walking somewhere. Often as not, he has linked his arm with mine as if to assure me in a tactile way of his support and friendship. It happened in many places—London, Paris, Berlin, Leipzig, and most often in Manhattan, as we were leaving one of our offices and going out to lunch. He had a favorite place on Forty-fifth Street where there were long tables that were shared with other guests, many obviously friends of his.

A key deRochemont associate, Lothar was the main producer for our *Martin Luther* movie. But then he went off to Indonesia to help set up a film program for the government there. On his return we re-connected.

It was Lothar who encouraged us to pursue the story of Johann Sebastian Bach as our next movie. He actually drafted a script (which was never used). But while researching that subject for us in Germany and in the Bach country of the then-Communist East Germany (Leipzig and all), Lothar and writer Allan Sloane discovered a more immediate story. They urged me and our board to have it produced as a movie even before Bach.

Because I worked so closely with Lothar, I was privy to his philosophy of life and his strong moral code. He was a film artist in Berlin and had to leave

Germany during the Nazi rise in Europe. After first fleeing to Denmark, he then came as a refugee to America, where as a new citizen he became a part of Louis deRochemont's team producing the popular *March of Time* cinema series. One striking memory for me was walking through the Jewish cemetery in East Berlin to the gravesite where his relatives were buried. It was at that moment I became aware of how important his Jewish roots were to him. He was probably the most cosmopolitan personality I've ever known. Elaine and I so enjoyed our social time with him and his wife Vee at our home, at their Forty-sixth Street apartment in New York, and at their northern Connecticut home.

I was proud to offer a eulogy at his memorial service. I miss Lothar very much.

Richard Solberg

Elaine and I always felt a warmth whenever we were together with Dick and his wife June. They complemented each other. She was jolly and effusive, an extrovert. Dick was the scholar, the serious, quiet, loving husband and father. Dick never realized how helpful he had been in my career. It was one of those osmosis situations: encounters with him influenced me. I was fascinated by him, and I respected and admired the evident solidarity of his character. Friendship with him was a gift.

For months before he died, Dick Solberg and I would try to speak every Friday by phone. I sensed he needed me as someone to share in his pain and frustration at being a caregiver. His wife June needed constant care. Dick found in me, I think, a person who understood what the physical and psychological pressures of caregiving were. Mostly I saw my role as being a good listener.

When he called, I would immediately know who it was by the sound of his voice. There was a recognizable "Solberg sound" in its resonant timbre. Describing audio impressions is not easy, but there is an unmistakable character in a Solberg voice. I think it has to do with the way vocal overtones overlap and are DNA-combined somehow. That distinctive quality has been genetically bequeathed to his progeny. One of Dick's sons is the well-known actor David Soul, who played Hutch in the *Starsky and Hutch* TV series decades ago. He has the "Solberg Sound" too, when he isn't inhabiting a role in a play or movie or television show.

Our careers, similar in some respects, were really very different. He was a well-respected historian. While we both had executive responsibilities in the church structure: his leadership was in education, and mine was communication. Yet, our paths crossed both professionally and socially, and we bonded back then in the decades before we both retired in the 1980s.

I felt affirmed by Dick every time we corresponded, talked by phone, or exchanged e-mails. I have all the books he has written. I particularly prize one; the memory of his voice and friendship seems to be embodied in that book's title—*As Between Brothers*.

A few months before he died in November of 2006, he sent me a note with a copy of a quote by the Danish philosopher Søren Kierkegaard. It had come from his brother Carl Solberg, a former editor at *Time* magazine. I treasure it more and more as I continue to write. Carl called it an "Epigraph for whatever we're writing."

Life can only be understood backwards; but it must be lived forwards.

My Wings at Sunset

From Salton Sea 1943
Words and music by Robert E. A. Lee

My wings at sun-set are far from your view.

My wings at sun-set are fly-ing for you.

The clouds be-yond me are part of my past.

My wings at sun-set come home now at last.

I'm tired and wea-ry from hours in the air.

I'll sleep and dream, dear, of to-mor-rows we will share.

My wings at sun-set o'er for-eign skies roam.

My wings at sun-set will car-ry me home!

Acknowledgments

My family has let me know that they are glad I have become passionate about writing. Their support has been magnificent.

Barbara Greenfeldt has proved to be a skilled editor. As she demonstrated with my two previous books, *Mathilda's Journey* and *Dear Elaine*, she is independent and thorough. At the same time she is professionally proficient in cleaning up my errant prose. All this—plus her insight into my life and legends as my daughter. She has my deepest gratitude, and I happily thank her.

I am grateful also to several who undertook to give me helpful reactions and suggestions from their reading of my manuscript. Novelist and playwright Robert Ford offered a bounty of constructive comments in a thorough professional review. Sylvia Lee-Thompson also, at my request that she be as objective as possible in spite of being my daughter, reviewed these pages before publication and provided a helpful critique.

Artist and designer daughter Peg Harris and her graphics designer husband Sherwin Harris have again collaborated to select and create the cover art and prepare the photo illustrations for publication, and I am deeply thankful to them.

I am indebted to high school friend Lois Langland, psychology professor retired from California's Scripps College, for permission to include her poem "Aging," which I found relevant to my own situation and appropriate as an epigraph for my story. My lyrics and music for the title song "My Wings at Sunset," as well as my original poems, are covered by copyright, while the hymn texts and the folk ballad "In the Gloaming" are in public domain. Photos of the Coronado seaplanes were provided by the U. S. Navy. Photos on the front and back cover are by Barbara Greenfeldt and used by permission. Other illustrations are from family archives.

These "sunset" days of being a retired widower are marked by my need for continuing creativity in my life. Writing supplies this, and I find I pursue it with zeal. This memoir has involved not only my own large and supportive family but also many friends who have encouraged me along the way through their visits, telephone calls, and e-mails.

The loving ghost of my wife of fifty-six years, Elaine, hovers over my life and labor in these years since she left us in October of the year 2000. She was my literary guide and critic throughout the years of our marriage. Echoes of her trenchant comments still guide my thinking.

I save most gratitude for the Lord whom I love and trust. Thank you, dear God.

ABOUT THE AUTHOR

Robert E. A. Lee, author of seven previous books, is a former communication chief for the Lutheran denomination in the United States. He has two feature movies and two major television documentaries to his credit as executive producer. Lee has been a TV host, syndicated radio movie critic, journalist, speech coach, and radio announcer and program director.

Since 1988 he has worked for his own organization, REALWorld Communications (www.realworldcomm.com), as a PR consultant and film maker. For religious relief and development organizations, Lee has produced educational videos in the Philippines, Tanzania, Kenya, Niger, Burkina Faso, India, Peru, and Honduras.

An essayist and poet, Lee has published his writings on his Internet Web site.

During World War II, he was a Navy seaplane pilot in the Pacific, surveying the waters for thousands of nautical miles surrounding the former Japanese-controlled islands from harbors in the Marshall, Mariana, and Okinawa chain of islands. The huge four-engine Coronado patrol bombers of his squadron were involved in searching for submarines and enemy shipping and even at times engaging in air combat with Japanese war planes. He was awarded the Navy's Distinguished Flying Cross.

Lee graduated from Luther College and did graduate study at the University of Minnesota and New York University. Susquehanna University honored him with a Doctor of Fine Arts degree.

During World War II he married Elaine Naeseth, a musician. During their fifty-six years of marriage, Elaine and Bob had six children. As adults, these four women and two men include a musician (Sigrid), an electronics engineer (Paul), a language educator (Barbara), a philosophy professor (Richard), a Lutheran pastor (Sylvia), and an artist and designer (Margaret). Elaine had been a teacher and organist. She was the subject of the seventh of his books, *Dear Elaine.*

Lee was born in 1921 and raised in Spring Grove, Minnesota. He is a resident of Baldwin, Long Island, New York.

978-0-595-44373-4
0-595-44373-7

Printed in the United States
93681LV00004B/301-363/A